Successful Terrariums

A Step-by-Step Guide

SUCCESSFUL TERRARIUMS

A Step-by-Step Guide

by

Ken Kayatta and Steven Schmidt

Black and white photography
by Steven Schmidt
Color photography by Thom DeSanto
Drawings by Lois Strasberg

A&W VISUAL LIBRARY

Lucille Ho
Oct 78

Library of Congress Catalog Card Number: 76-9938
ISBN: 0-89104-048-X
Published by arrangement with Houghton Mifflin Company
Boston, Massachusetts
Manufactured in the United States of America

Acknowledgments

We would like to thank Nancy Holmes for her initial and continuing encouragement and interest in this book, Frances Tenenbaum for her many suggestions and editing ability, Brian Woolf for hours and hours in the darkroom, and dozens of friends and neighbors who offered suggestions, gave advice, and tested our planting procedures and instructions.

Contents

Introduction

1 The Origin, Theory, and Enjoyment of Terrariums

Have you ever looked in a florist's window and wondered how those full-grown plants got inside that narrow-necked bottle? Would you like plants in your home that require almost no attention, take care of themselves while you are away on vacation, and always look healthy? Does the idea of making inexpensive, unusual gifts appeal to you? Would you enjoy a hobby that sets up a segment of nature, complete with plants and even animals, right in your living room? If you said "yes" to any of those questions, terrariums are for you.

What is a terrarium? Strictly speaking, a terrarium is a clear, sealed container in which plants are grown in a moisture-balanced environment. We describe a wide variety of these in this book, including bottle gardens, but we also include related projects, like desert plantings and vivariums, which are similarly constructed but should not be sealed. We use "terrarium" in a general way to mean plants growing in a container, but when we talk about "terrarium theory" we mean the moisture-balanced environment that occurs only in a closed, clear container.

The ideal terrarium is an attractive, maintenance-free, miniature scene from nature. The plants grow slowly and evenly in a soil mix that is not overly rich, but provides proper nutrients. Temperature and light conditions are exactly right for all of the plants in the container; the moisture level is constant and self-perpetuating. This book is planned to

3

A coffee table terrarium — a showpiece that is useful, attractive, and a constant source of pleasure

A bottle garden requires special tools, special techniques, and a steady hand

help you achieve these goals. Perfection may not always be reached, but with our guidelines you should have both success and fun. You will certainly have many beautiful collections of greenery safe from foliage-nibbling cats, curious puppies, and inquisitive hands.

Although the most enjoyable part of the terrarium experience is selecting the elements, creating the design, and planting the miniature scene, terrarium building involves more than putting some plants in an attractive container. Almost any procedure will produce a terrarium that looks O.K. at first. But unless you provide the essentials necessary for a long and prosperous life, your terrarium will soon develop troubles. To be successful, you must combine a liking for plants with an understanding of their needs. As an example, watering a terrarium that doesn't look well may show your interest and concern, but it may also give the coup de grâce to already drowning plants. This book is planned to help you understand everything you need to know to create and maintain healthy, happy terrariums. We think that will make you healthier and happier, too.

With the instructions in this book, you can assemble a terrarium in thirty minutes, or take several days. You can spend a couple of dollars for

4 • *Introduction*

simple plants, or much more for exotic ones. You can use an empty pickle jar or a crystal decanter for a container. Once you start building terrariums you'll want to share them with others. Your handcrafted gift will mean much more than anything you can purchase. We like to keep two or three simple terrariums on hand for impromptu presents, for a relative who unexpectedly lands in the hospital, to say hello to a new neighbor, or just for a sudden burst of friendship.

For a young child you might put in a natural-looking small animal, give it a name, and make up a story about its life. We recommended this to a friend, whose young niece Jane was down with the flu. Jane's present was a small woodland terrarium containing a little ceramic beaver named Chomp-Chomp, portrayed as a playful chap who liked to waddle around the forest and build dams with his fellow beavers.

A few weeks later our friend dropped by, having almost forgotten about Chomp-Chomp. But not Jane, who proudly showed off her prospering terrarium and told several amusing tales of the beaver's adventures. Chomp-Chomp and his forest had become part of her life, and perhaps the seeds for a future terrarium and nature lover had been sown.

Terrariums make excellent nature-study projects for children, who take great delight in watching their plants grow and prosper, and learn a good deal about botany and ecology in the process. Older children and teen-agers can build any of the terrariums we describe if they follow the procedures carefully. Even very young children can be introduced to terrariums by letting them help you stir up the ingredients that make up the soil mix, or place a few rocks in the completed planting. Vivariums are fascinating to youngsters, but must be considered a full-fledged

Chomp-Chomp, a beaver, inhabits
this children's woodland terrarium
inside a two-quart storage jar
from Anchor Hocking

For a money-saving, change-of-pace centerpiece, use a few of your terrariums

hobby, not a simple project, for the animals in them require care and responsibility.

On special occasions it's fun to move your small and medium-sized terrariums to a more prominent location. Use them to decorate a coffee table or as the centerpiece for a dining table. A group of them is effective on a buffet or mantel. And the plants will probably enjoy the extra attention, because we firmly believe that plants like to be liked. There is much research on this to be done, but some studies indicate that plants may have emotions and reactions. It even appears that they respond to conversation, enjoy music, and can tell when someone really doesn't like them. We can't promise that communicating with your plants will make you a plant wizard, but it certainly can't do any harm.

How Terrariums Originated

To look at a terrarium you might imagine that it was specifically designed as an attractive way to display a grouping of plants. In fact, it developed from a lucky accident that happened to a man keen enough to recognize it as a breakthrough in natural science. This accident not only led to terrariums, but to a method of transporting plants that changed agriculture and botany around the world.

Although we think of air pollution as a current problem, in the 1820s the furnaces and factories of the Industrial Revolution had made much of England's city air, in the words of a contemporary, "filthy and unfit to breathe." Living in London at that time was a surgeon named Dr. Nathaniel Ward, whose hobby was natural history. In 1829 he began an experiment with the cocoon of a sphinx moth. To study the hatching of the adult, he placed the cocoon in moist earth inside a sealed bottle. Much to his surprise, some grass and a tiny fern began growing out of the damp soil — the same fern the doctor had been unsuccessfully trying to grow in his garden. Since he had blamed air pollution for his failure, he deduced that within his bottle the fumes of London had no effect.

Dr. Ward proceeded to concentrate on other experiments involving plants in sealed containers. His most significant achievement was the development of large glass containers to ship plants around the world, allowing them to survive long sea and rail trips. In his first test, he shipped two cases of grasses and ferns to Australia. The plants remained on deck for the long sea journey and arrived in fine health. Ward's results were published in 1842, and the glass containers were promptly dubbed "Wardian cases." Tea plants from Shanghai were shipped to India; young rubber trees went from Brazil to Ceylon; Chinese banana trees were shipped to Fiji and the Samoan Islands.

A worldwide boom also developed within horticultural circles. Wardian cases were used to exchange plants and stock botanical gardens with many new specimens. Conservatories in wealthy homes and greenhouses all over the Victorian world displayed collections of exotic and tropical plants. Many of these varieties are still enjoyed today as popular house plants or in public botanical gardens.

The doctor's discovery also led to the Victorian craze for home versions of the Wardian case, smaller, often intricately designed containers intended as showpieces for the parlor and drawing room. These direct ancestors of today's terrariums contained ferns, mosses, and small tropical plants. The great vogue for the ornamental cases eventually ran its course and terrariums became mainly of interest as schoolroom projects, for laboratory study, and the occasional rare hobbyist.

Today a terrarium boom is taking place which exceeds even that of a century ago. We no longer consider a terrarium a curiosity or an experiment, but a means of bringing nature and plants into our lives. The simple pleasure of nurturing and enjoying plants in our homes seems to bring joy to more people every day. Plastic plants certainly do not satisfy the need for carefree indoor greenery, but terrariums may.

As you will see, we emphasize a natural approach to terrariums. We like to use natural materials in a natural way to create a natural scene — a section of a woodland, tropical, or desert environment. Terrariums loaded with purple gravel, plush bunny rabbits, and plastic flowers make our stomachs turn. If these tasteless horrors are the only kind you have seen, a special pleasure awaits you in creating a terrarium from natural elements. The compliment we look for on a finished planting is "How great!" not "How cute!"

These terrariums revive the feeling
of Victorian "Wardian Cases"

This woodland environment re-creates a scene from
a forest floor in Ambassador's 5½-gallon aquarium

How a Terrarium Works

Why are all those little plants inside a terrarium so green and healthy? That's easy — because they are living in a happy home, one that provides ideal surroundings that duplicate the conditions of their natural home. To understand the terrarium operation, it is necessary to review a few basic principles of plant life and growth. All you really need to know is *what* happens, not the scientific wiggles of *how*.

Can you quickly name the basic elements needed for plant life? The easy ones are a growing medium, light, and water. The ones you might not recall are carbon dioxide, nutrients, and proper drainage. In nature a plant that doesn't have a favorable combination of these elements grows poorly or not at all. But humans like to tinker, and we are able to grow plants throughout the world for food and pleasure by artificially duplicating their natural growing conditions. We often make improvements by the elimination of harmful insects and diseases, the use of soil additives, and by hybridization. A successful terrarium involves the same principles; it depends on how nearly you can duplicate, or even improve upon, a plant's natural home.

One natural condition you will create is a miniature version of the water cycle that occurs throughout the world. When water evaporates into the air, it rises, cools, and eventually falls to the earth as rain to stimulate plant growth. In your terrarium the same process will be duplicated, except that you won't be treated to indoor rainstorms. Instead, the rain showers will simply be condensed droplets of moisture which collect on the top and sides of the terrarium and eventually fall or drop back to the surface and the plants. The sure sign of a properly balanced terrarium is a slight misting of its top or sides.

A question that will come up when your friends see your closed terrarium is "Don't the plants need air to live?" Of course they do, specifically the carbon dioxide found in the air. But don't worry, they need very little and even a closed terrarium isn't airtight. The moisture will be trapped inside, but a little air will always be seeping in and out. It's a good idea to open the lid or take out the cork once a week for a few minutes and say "Hello" to the plants inside. This will given them some

Nature's Water Cycle: Water evaporates, rises, becomes rain, and falls to give plants needed moisture

A Terrarium's Water Cycle: Water evaporates from leaves and the soil surface, rises, condenses on the container sides, and falls to provide moisture for the plants

new air and carbon dioxide without upsetting the moisture balance.

Photosynthesis is the word used to describe the way green plants use energy from the sun to produce their own food. In this process, carbon dioxide, which is present in the air, reacts with the water brought to the green parts of the plant from its roots. The result is the production of carbohydrates, in the form of sugars and starches. Chlorophyll is the mysterious green pigment in plants that makes this conversion possible. A by-product of the food-production process is oxygen, which is released into the air by the plant. You noticed, of course, that this is exactly the reverse of what happens in animals, including us — we take in oxygen, use it to maintain life, and expel carbon dioxide. With these two operations we have another important cycle, the one between plants and animals.

Open your terrarium occasionally and say "Hello"

That's the end of the botany lesson; knowing these things is a part of truly understanding life in your terrarium. Now we are ready to move on to what this book is really about — creating successful and beautiful terrariums.

A hanging terrarium
in a 12-inch globe from
Riekes Crisa

2 Selecting Your First Terrarium Project

Now that you understand how a terrarium works, it's time to get into action. Your first steps involve only mental work, so relax and pour yourself a cup of coffee or a drink (depending on the time of day and your taste). Before you decide which is your best first project, you need to evaluate your experience with plants, consider possible terrarium locations, and match these with a terrarium environment. If you do this carefully, the result will be success in your first undertaking, and that's the best way we can think of to make you a terrarium fan.

First, we have a three-part quiz to help you rate yourself as an indoor gardener. Simply stated, it asks "How good and how experienced are you with plants?" Remember we have something for everyone, whether you have a black thumb or greenery that turns others green with envy, so no cheating. What's important is to evaluate your ability fairly and then pick the right project.

This simple, first terrarium can be
built with no previous experience

Beginner. Consider yourself a beginning terrarium builder if most of
the following are true:

1. I have never built a terrarium.

2. I pick up a plant or two at a store no more than occasionally, and
once in a while they don't live.

3. I have never repotted a plant or made my own soil mix.

4. I've had only easy-to-grow plants like philodendron, ivy, or a snake
plant or I haven't the slightest idea what they are called.

5. I have not kept plants around the house until the past year.

If you said "not true" to all of those, congratulations and move on to the
Intermediate Quiz. If you said "true," don't despair because we have a
sure-fire success for you in chapter 6 and nothing builds confidence like
winning the first time out. So skip the next two quizzes and go on
reading.

Intermediate. Consider yourself an intermediate terrarium builder if
most of the following are true:

1. I have built only one or two terrariums.

2. I have been successful with only about ten or twelve plants in my
home.

3. I have read not more than two or three books on house plants or
indoor gardening.

4. I have not yet planted a narrow-neck terrarium or used artificial
growing lights.

5. I have had house plants around only for one or two years.

If you said "not true" to all of those, give yourself a pat on the back,
refill your cup or glass, and try the Advanced Quiz. If you said "true" to
three or more, the first-time terrarium in chapter 6 is still a good place
to start. It will give you more experience in working with plants in a
container before you move on to more challenging terrariums.

Advanced. Consider yourself an advanced terrarium builder if most of the following are true:

1. I have successfully constructed more than two terrariums.

2. I have been involved with house plants or indoor gardening for more than two years.

3. I have experimented with a wide range of plants or many within my special interest field, i.e., African violets, cacti, or ferns.

4. I have read several books on house plants and indoor gardening.

5. I have done repotting and know my plants' needs as to soil mix, light, and water.

If you said "true" to all or most of those, you are going to have a ball with this book. Be sure to read all the chapters in Part I, and then either follow the step-by-step first-time planting for a review or choose an intermediate project. You are probably itching to try a narrow-neck terrarium, so go ahead. Then you can move on to large containers or any advanced project.

An advanced project such as a bottle on its side requires experience and patience. Everything except the plants comes in a kit from Garden in a Bottle

Terrarium Size and Location

Are you still sitting there doing your mental work? Good, because now you are ready for your next decision — what and where. There are hundreds of possible terrarium containers and places to put them. Let your imagination run free as you look around the room and decide where you would like to see a really super looking terrarium. Consider coffee tables, end tables, bookshelves, and even the floor for larger bottles. You'll probably find several good locations. Now ask yourself what kind of terrarium would look best in each of these places. For example, a terrarium on a coffee table should be rather small and not easily upset; one on a bookshelf could be larger.

If you decide on a hanging terrarium, find a location out of heavy traffic patterns and slightly below eye level so you can get right next to it and look in. Just below eye level is also best for aquarium containers. You're going to get lots of comments and questions from visitors, so find a spot that displays your creation to its best advantage. Container selection is discussed in the next chapter, so for now just look around for a possible location and an approximate size.

Light, as you know, is a plant essential. As you're casting around the room for terrarium sites, consider the amount of light each location receives. If you have a spot that receives bright light, but not direct sun, for two thirds of the day, you have a terrarium heaven.

A general guide to indoor light levels and the kind of terrariums that will flourish in each is given on the following page.

All of these conditions omit the use of artificial lighting. Fortunately, you are no longer tied to natural light. We'll talk more about lights later, but for the present you can plan to use any location that receives additional light from a table or floor lamp to compensate for lack of natural light. We even have one terrarium, with very undemanding plants, thriving in a cellar TV room underneath a 60-watt table light turned on for twelve hours a day.

17

An étagère of terrariums can be used
to display a variety of plantings

Sunny: an unobstructed east, south, or west window. Excellent for desert terrariums; unacceptable for woodland or tropical terrariums

Bright light: an obstructed (filtered sunlight or light shade) east, south, or west window; or up to 5 feet away from a sunny window. Excellent for woodland and tropical terrariums; acceptable for desert

Medium light: from 5 to 12 feet away from a sunny window; or up to 5 feet away from a bright-light window; or an unobstructed north window. Acceptable for woodland and tropical terrariums

Low light: from 12 to 18 feet away from a sunny window; or 5 to 10 feet away from a bright-light window. Acceptable for woodland or tropical terrariums, but with the use of low-light plants

The Three Terrarium Environments

Three distinct miniature environments are discussed throughout the book, each with its own appearance and requirements. Plants from the three should not be mixed. Trying to grow a cactus and a fern together means that one of the plants is going to die. Some tropical and woodland plant requirements do overlap, and occasionally these can be used together.

Tropical. This grouping might also be called "general foliage" and is drawn from popular house plants found in stores all over the country. They are very easy to work with and quite tolerant of the whims of humans and of nature. If you are a beginning or intermediate terrarium builder, a tropical terrarium is best for your first few projects. Mixing the plants in this category is easy and a close grouping is used to produce a lush effect. Mass-produced versions intended for quick sale often contain brightly colored gravel and elves to "liven" them up, which gives us instant diarrhea. You can easily produce better ones by taking the time to design and plant with care, and adding natural elements such as small rocks, sand, and wood chips to complete the look of nature.

Woodland. In this, the most naturalistic of the three environments, the aim is to create a scene from the forest floor or a cool woodland area. Your

The tropical environment is a blend of plant colors and textures

The woodland environment emphasizes ferns, forest plants, and lush greens

A desert environment uses a sparse, open
feeling to re-create an arid, dry scene

terrarium will contain ferns, moss, and other moisture-loving woodland plants, with pebbles, seed pods, twigs, acorns, lichen, and other fascinating pieces collected from nature. The use of banked areas and different levels will heighten the realism. This environment is most effective in a rectangular aquarium, but can be produced in many other containers.

Desert. Just about everything in this environment is different from the other two — plants, soil mix, light requirements, moisture, and — most important of all — no cover. A closed container would be too humid for these plants, which are cacti and succulents. The desired look is that of a desert setting. These plants come from arid or semi-arid regions of the world and grow in a dry, sandy soil.

The natural elements in a desert terrarium will be rocks, dried branches, thistle pods, sand, and pebbles. There will be more bare ground and the soil mix will be a lighter color because of its composition and dryness. A desert terrarium thrives in direct sun, but can adapt to bright light if necessary. Since the water cycle is not in effect, the plants need to be watered, but because they like to be very dry between waterings, maintenance is easy. This environment is so special we have devoted a separate chapter to it: "The Wonderful World of Cacti and Succulents."

Now it's time to pick your terrarium container.

3 Terrarium Containers

"Terrarium container" is an all-encompassing term for what will hold your plants. There are so many possible containers that you may come up with an idea no one else ever imagined. The only material we recommend for a closed terrarium is glass, but after that the choice is up to you, as long as the container has three important qualities:

First, it must be moisture proof. If not, the interior will dry out and the water cycle will be broken. For some containers this means that you will have to add a top, but this is very easy.

Second, the container must be transparent, which means clear. This, of course, is to allow maximum light to reach the plants. Light tints are often used for bottle gardens, and the tropical plants used for these terrariums are not noticeably affected. Darker tints should not be used, because they greatly reduce the available light and make the plants almost impossible to see.

The third requirement seems obvious, but make sure your container is the right size. How do you know what that is? There are marvelous terrarium containers from very tiny decorative jars to large aquariums that weigh 80 pounds or more when planted. To decide on the right container, consider where it will be placed, what effect you want to achieve, and if the weight of the completed project is enough to make it a consideration. It is also *very* important that you allow room inside the container for plant growth.

Some samples of the range of possible terrarium containers

Food jars can be "recycled"
into terrarium containers

If you have a container on hand, you will want to choose plants to fit it; if you start with the plants, you will need to find a suitable container. A gift terrarium will have to be portable and you will probably want to use a decorative jar. On a sudden impulse you may spot a container and buy it because you know it will make a great terrarium. All of these are "right" terrarium containers if they are properly planted and located.

There are several ways to provide tops for containers that come without them. A decorative top can sometimes be bought separately, or you can use a plain glass plate. If you can't find one, any glazier will cut a piece of clear glass to your exact specifications, including tops for round containers. Smaller openings can be covered with $\frac{1}{16}$-inch glass, but aquariums need $\frac{1}{8}$-inch or $\frac{3}{16}$-inch. All of these tops will provide the

To find containers,
think terrarium thoughts

moisture-proofing you need to establish the rain cycle. As a temporary measure you can use transparent food wrap, but it isn't very attractive and should be replaced as soon as possible.

To find free terrarium containers in your home all you have to do is think terrarium thoughts. Open your refrigerator or pantry and see what you have on hand. Think carefully before you throw away any glass container; for years you have probably been putting potential terrariums in the garbage can. Now you know better and all you have to do is convert them from their present use, or non-use, to a new one. You can even visit your local bottle-recycling center to find the best free terrarium containers in the whole neighborhood.

Keep your eyes open for glass jars that once held such items as instant coffee, fruit juice, mayonnaise, chilled fruit, or peanut butter. These come in a wide range of sizes, and the largest will be the easiest to plant. Look for the widest openings you can find. If you are choosing a container for your first terrarium, make sure you can reach inside. Don't overlook small jars, as they can make charming miniature terrariums with only one or two plants and some moss.

In the kitchen you may also find glass refrigerator-storage jars, cookie or cracker jars, canisters, and many other containers that meet your three basic requirements. Wine or cider bottles with a neck opening of 2½ inches or less fall into the category called "narrow-neck," which really means "rough to plant." We have a special chapter on how to plant these, but we will also tell you how to cut them in two for easier planting.

A one-gallon food jar,
before and after

Many food jars have brightly colored tops, often with labeling, that
should be covered with a few squirts of brown or green spray paint. This
makes them much more attractive and they will blend in with your
natural look.

Don't limit yourself to the kitchen. Elsewhere in the house you may
find an unused fishbowl or aquarium, a decorative brandy snifter, a
decanter, or an apothecary jar which can be given a new lease on life by
becoming a terrarium. By now you can see that terrarium containers are
lurking everywhere, so use your imagination to discover them.

If you don't have a thing in the house for your terrarium to wear, you
can go shopping for one. You will find them everywhere, from supermarket to dime store to the swankiest gift shop in town. Check the
housewares section of any variety, discount, or department store. Garden
centers and plant stores often have a wide range of containers specifically
for terrariums. Visit a tropical fish store for aquariums. Don't overlook
kitchen or other specialty supply stores for unusual items. Secondhand or
even junk shops can produce real beauties at bargain prices. One of our
favorite containers is an antique medicine bottle found jumbled in with a
lot of second-rate glass and china in a charity thrift shop.

At this point we should tell you why we do not recommend Plexiglas, Lucite, or other plastic containers for *closed* woodland and tropical terrariums. The reasons are:

1. Water does not run down the sides but tends to fog up the entire container, making it difficult to see the interior. If the plastic container has an opening this does not occur, but then you lose the humidity, moisture balance, and easy maintenance of a closed terrarium.

2. In glued (as opposed to molded) containers, the humidity can create warping, which may cause the seams to split and ruin both the container and the terrarium.

3. The design of many mass-marketed plastic containers can only be described as tacky. A well-designed supermarket bottle is often twice as attractive.

4. Plastic containers must be handled and cleaned carefully as they scratch easily.

Some of the many containers specially designed for terrariums

Narrow-neck containers require special planting procedures

On the other hand, if you find an attractive plastic container and decide it is perfect for a specific idea, go ahead and use it. Remember that it cannot be sealed, so both misting and watering will be necessary. In addition, we can heartily recommend plastic containers for desert terrariums. These terrariums are not closed, have no moisture cycle, and look great in well-designed plastic containers.

In your shopping you may also run across terrarium kits. There are many already available and new ones come out frequently, so it is impossible to evaluate them all. In general, if plants are included you should avoid them. Some kits offer a container, drainage material, charcoal, soil mix, and even tools. They can save you a lot of steps, but compare the price with the convenience and decide if you are getting a good value.

Kit instructions are often greatly simplified, especially in the area of plant selection. To make the most of your kit, use the plant selection guide and planting procedures recommended in this book. It's impossible to give blanket advice on the soil mix found in kits, but the ones we have seen could benefit from the addition of a soil lightener and peat moss, plus a little humus if you are making a woodland planting. Soil mixes will be thoroughly covered in the next chapter, so you will be able to evaluate kit mixes better after reading that.

A hanging terrarium is an especially attractive way to display your plants. Obviously there are limitations on the size and shape of the container and its location. Glass bubble balls, chemist's flasks, decorative round-bottom bottles, wine bottles, and other containers in the spherical or egg-shaped category work best. Flat-bottomed and rectangular shapes are not as satisfactory.

The third way to obtain a terrarium container is to make your own. We have three favorites — cut bottles, glass rectangles, and (for desert terrariums) plastic rectangles.

Bottle-cutting makes it possible for you to lift off the top of a bottle, plant a terrarium, and replace the top for the look of a narrow-neck container without using a special planting procedure. It also permits the use of plants that would never fit into a narrow-neck bottle, such as miniature African violets. To be honest, it takes a little practice and you'll probably lose a few bottles at first. Just remember to save some bottles for trial runs before you start on your best one. Of the several methods available, we think the one called "scribe and tap" is the easiest. You have probably seen it demonstrated on television or in a store. It uses a glass cutter attached to a frame to scribe or cut a thin line around the bottle, and a long metal gadget to tap along this line from inside the bottle to complete the break.

Bottle cutting allows you to create a narrow-neck look without special planting tools

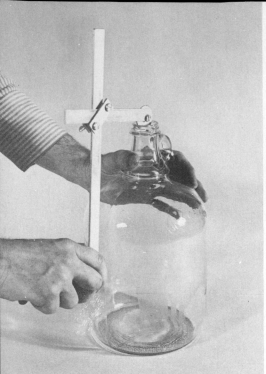  

First, a cutting apparatus is used to scribe a line around the bottle. A tapper is used to complete the break. The bottom is easily planted, and the top goes back on

Bottle-cutting kits are readily available in department and dime stores. If possible borrow one from a friend. Kits come with full instructions, and all you need is a little practice to get the hang of the operation. Here are three tips that will make the cutting easier:

1. Make sure the upright part of the frame is exactly vertical and all angles are exactly 90° before you tighten the bolts.

2. Try to turn the bottle as smoothly as possible, using even pressure on the cutting frame. You are just making a thin line, not cutting through the bottle. Don't recut over the line. If you see a spot that didn't get cut, go over that spot only.

3. To complete the break, tap gently at first and gradually increase the motion. The pendulumlike movement for tapping is the most difficult to master. Thickness of glass can vary within one bottle as well as from bottle to bottle, and overenthusiasm may result in a cracked bottle, so try this on a few practice bottles first.

If you are going to reassemble the bottle, do not smooth the cut edges. Use a small piece of tape or grease pencil to mark the alignment of the two halves. When the top is replaced, your bottle will be moisture proof, and the cut will be almost invisible. Don't forget to replace the cork. To use only the bottom as a desert planter, smooth the cut edge with the paper provided in the kit, "wet and dry" paper, or emery paper.

Assembling a glass cube will not save you much money, but will give you the flexibility to make any size container you want, and not having a metal or plastic supporting frame produces a clean, modern look. It is especially recommended for a coffee-table terrarium. Once you learn the technique and get used to the smell of the adhesive, working with glass is easy. Always work with someone; in this project one step needs four hands.

To assemble a 12-inch cube you will need:

Cleaning materials — glass cleaner, paper towels, single-edged razor
    blade, and steel wool
Six pieces of ¼-inch glass, with ends polished:
        Top and bottom — two pieces, 12 x 12 inches
        Long sides   — two pieces, 12 x 12 inches
        Short sides   — two pieces, 12 x 11½ inches
One miter-band kit, consisting of four corner pieces, a tightening
    band and a wrench made by Adjustable Clamp Company, avail-
    able at large hardware stores.
Rubber-based glass adhesive, available at tropical fish stores, glass-
    supply stores, or hardware stores
5-foot piece of light cord

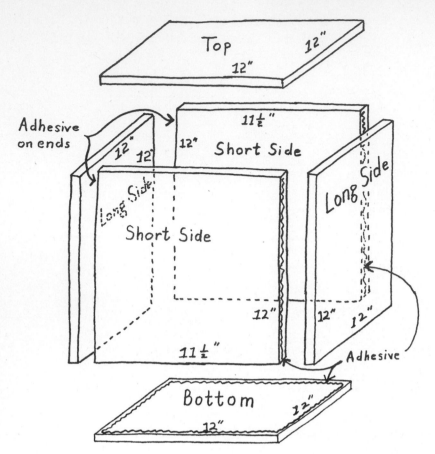

Top 12"
12"

Adhesive on ends

12" 12"

11½"
12" Short Side

Long Side

Short Side

12" 12" 12"

11½"

Adhesive

Bottom 12"
12"

Glass cube assembly: Note where the adhesive is to be placed and names of parts

Construct your glass cube in an out-of-the-way place where it can sit forty-eight hours to dry. Put down a layer of newspaper to protect the surface from spilled adhesive. Read through all of the instructions and study the cube diagram before starting. Then follow these steps:

1. Assemble all of your materials on the work space. Use glass cleaner to remove all dust and grease from the areas where adhesive is to be applied. See diagram for these areas.

2. Lay the bottom on the work space and fit the metal corner pieces under the four corners. Lay the tightening band around the corner pieces, but do not put tension on it.

3. Place adhesive around the perimeter of the bottom, as close to the edge as possible and in a solid line about ¼-inch wide.

a. The adhesive is first applied around the perimeter of the bottom piece. *b.* Positioning the sides requires two people

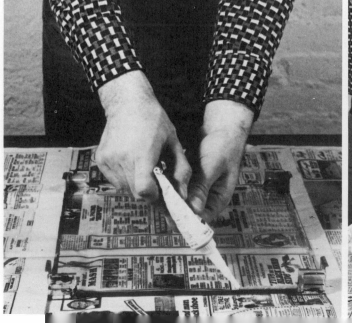
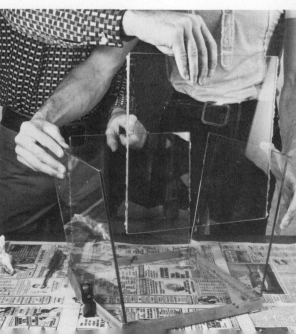

4. Put adhesive on the *ends* of the short sides. This is the edge that measures 12 inches, not the one that measures 11½ inches (see diagram). Lay the first side on a box or book while you do the second side. Then place the second side on a box while you carry out step 5.

5. This step needs the help of your partner. Place the first long side in position on the bottom, fitting it into the corner pieces. Have your helper hold it while you position the second long side. Have him hold that steady also. Both should be tilted outward very slightly, about 15°.

6. Take the first short side and put it into position between the two long sides. It should stay in position by itself, or your partner can steady it if necessary. Do *not* straighten the long sides at this point. Place the second short side, *then* bring the long sides to a vertical position to form a cube. Make sure the top corners are aligned properly.

7. Place the band into position around the corner braces and tighten it with the wrench as described on the miter-band kit box. Push each bottom corner of the short sides outward to make sure they are in position.

8. To hold the top corners in position, use a piece of cord. Tie it tightly with your helper's assistance. You can tighten it with a tourniquet method if necessary, using a pencil or small screwdriver.

9. Check to make sure all corners, top and bottom, are in position. Push the short sides out to line up with the long sides if necessary.

10. Allow the cube to dry for forty-eight hours, then remove the clamps and cord. Scrape off excess adhesive with a single-edged razor blade. Stubborn spots can be touched up with fine or medium grade steel wool. Give the entire cube a good cleaning before you begin to plant.

c. After the band has been tightened around the bottom, cord can be used to tighten the top. *d.* Completed cube, planted with a woodland scene

To make a glass rectangle of the dimensions you wish, simply adjust the dimensions of the sides and of the top and bottom in proportion. For example, a rectangle 16 inches long, 10 inches wide, and 11 inches high would have:

Top and bottom — two pieces, 16 x 10 inches
Long sides   — two pieces, 16 x 11 inches
Short sides   — two pieces, 9½ x 11 inches

For a coffee table terrarium, the top should be made from ⅜-inch glass. Allow at least 3½ to 4 inches extra on each side. This means that the top will measure 7 to 8 inches larger than the bottom in *both* directions, or about 23 x 17 inches in the example above.

Assembling a plastic cube or rectangle is very similar to making one with glass. We will note the differences, and you can put the container together following the same ten steps.

1. Since plastic (Lucite, Plexiglas, or other named brand) is recommended only for desert terrariums, no top is needed. (A closed plastic rectangle will be constantly fogged and will probably warp.)

2. Two methods are available for attaching the parts. The aquarium

A plastic container is taped, then a special solvent is used to fasten the sides together, and a desert scene is planted inside

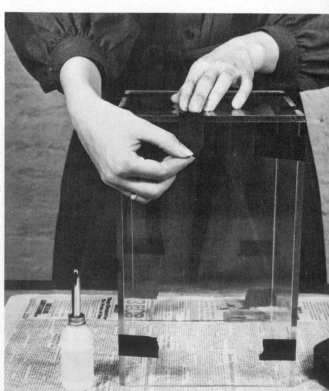

sealer used for glass containers can be used, in which case the miter band should be used to steady the sides and hold them while they dry. A special plastic solvent can also be used. This causes the areas where it is applied to "melt" and "refreeze" almost instantly, and is applied with a special needled applicator or an eyedropper. With this method no banding is necessary, but the cube pieces must be *exactly* in position as they cannot be moved after the solvent is applied. Use masking tape to assemble the cube; seal the corners from the inside with the plastic solvent. Although the bond is instant, let the cube stand an hour or so to dry thoroughly.

3. For containers up to a two-gallon capacity, material ³⁄₁₆-inch thick is good; larger containers should be made from ¼-inch. This can be cut to size at plastic supply houses or at the hobby shops and craft centers which sell it. If you want to buy a large sheet and cut it yourself, you will need a fine-toothed saw or saw blade, which is available at plastic specialty and hardware stores. Rough edges should be sanded with a medium (60-to-80) paper before glueing.

4. Be very careful when working with and cleaning plastic as it scratches much more easily than glass. A special cleaner is available, which is a combination of anti-static, cleaner, and polish.

For a long, healthy life, *all* terrariums are dependent upon adequate drainage and a correctly proportioned soil mix

4 Soil Mixes and Drainage

This chapter is for all of you who mixed up mud pies as a kid. You're going to have a chance to do it all over again, with recipes but without water. Soggy mud pies are O.K. for kids, but for terrarium planting you want a barely moist, workable mixture.

First let's get our definitions straight. Soil is what you use for planting; dirt is what you sweep off the floor. Please don't confuse the two. Plants grow in a soil mix, which is a combination of soil and other ingredients. In everyday conversation we often say "soil" when we really mean a properly constituted "soil mix," but we will try to keep the terms separate in this book. Plants are fairly tolerant of soil conditions in the short run, but for continued health they must have a balanced soil mix and adequate drainage.

The beauty of a terrarium is what you see above the surface. Beneath the surface are five elements that produce this beauty and are the foundation for a healthy terrarium, as shown in this diagram.

Plant Roots

Soil Mix

Soil Separator

Charcoal

Drainage

We will discuss these elements in the order in which you place them, from the bottom upward. (Except for roots, which obviously cannot be discussed as separate entities from the plants.)

Drainage is needed in the bottom of all terrariums; both its function and appearance must be considered. Plants can't stand having their roots in water, and the drainage layer will make sure they never do. In nature, when rain falls the moisture that does not evaporate or become absorbed into plant roots drains into the subsoil. In a closed environment this system cannot operate, and it's up to you to supply a substitute.

The best drainage is a fine (¼-inch) to medium (½-inch) gravel. Anything much larger tends to be too coarse and looks out of scale. Color is very important. Pink, blue and green are out; natural colors are in! We like a rough-textured look in brown, tan, gray, black, or brick red, but it really depends on what's available in your area. Small pebbles or rocks can also be used.

In very decorative containers white gravel works well, but not in a naturalistic setting, which should utilize earth tones. Mix white and gray for a more natural but still decorative effect. In a hanging terrarium you can reduce the weight by using pulverized feather rock or pumice. Both are very lightweight, but hard to find in small quantities. If you have access to some, it's fine for all plantings.

How much drainage do you need? It's impossible to get too much, as far as function goes, but limited space and appearance are important. A good rule of thumb is to have one-third drainage and two-thirds soil mix. This refers to depth, not volume, so the shape of your container can have an effect on the amount you use. Make sure there is room for any excess water in the drainage level; ½ inch is about the minimum; 1½ inches should be enough for even the largest container.

Samples of drainage
material, actual size

If a container has straight sides, place it on top of the material while cutting the soil separator

With sloping sides, use a trial-and-error method. For a circle, fold cloth three times and cut like this

Charcoal in your terrarium absorbs odors and keeps the entire planting smelling sweet. It's the same stuff used to grill steaks, but you need enough for a field-mouse barbecue. You can actually use crushed barbecue charcoal if you want, but we recommend that you buy a small package of "horticultural grade charcoal." It's very cheap, much cleaner, and good to have around for all indoor gardening.

For very small terrariums, 3 inches or so in diameter, you can omit the gravel and use horticultural charcoal as your drainage material.

A *soil separator* is used to keep the soil mix from settling or sifting into the drainage layer, which would considerably destroy its function. Sounds simple, but very few terrarium builders have ever heard of such a device. We use it in every one of our terrariums and consider it as essential as any other subsurface element. It lies right over the drainage and charcoal and should be cut to barely touch the sides of the container.

The soil separator must be made from a synthetic material. Since it is in constant contact with the soil mix, organic matter could easily rot out. It must be porous enough to allow water to pass through easily, fine enough to hold back soil-mix particles. Fiber-glass drapery material is the best and is very cheap. Other suggestions are a nylon stocking, discarded curtains, old dress material, or rustproof metal screening. Color is unimportant as the soil separator should not be visible in the completed terrarium; to be safe, avoid bright colors and look for earth tones.

Soil Mixes

A good soil mix for terrarium planting is a combination of ingredients that provides adequate moisture retention, good drainage, nutrients, proper consistency, and an oxygen supply. Different plants have different needs so we provide a recipe for each environment. First, let's discuss the ingredients since our recipes may have some that are new to you.

Soil is what some of you once called dirt. Terrarium soil means only one thing — sterilized potting soil, which comes packaged and is available wherever plants and gardening supplies are sold. Basically it is a rich loam that has been sterilized to rid it of insects, insect eggs, fungus, and bacteria, and screened to produce a fine texture. It is often enriched with humus or other organic matter, and in this case should say so on the label. Any soil called "general purpose potting soil" or "house plant soil" is fine. Swiss Farms and Black Magic are both excellent and widely available. Make sure you don't get a special purpose soil mixture, such as cactus or African violet soil.

If you have great garden soil and don't mind stinking up your kitchen, you can make your own sterilized soil. First run it through a window screen or something a bit more open to remove sticks, pebbles, and other unwanted matter. Preheat the oven to 200° and put the soil either in a roasting pan lined with aluminum foil or in a roasting bag. Keep it 1 to 2 inches deep at most. Pop it in the oven for an hour. Once you have tried this you will probably decide that garden soil belongs in the garden and buying the small amount needed for terrariums is a good idea.

Peat moss is the decomposed remains of plants and is used to loosen the soil, make it more moisture-retentive, and provide roughage for plant roots. It comes in sizes from 6 cubic feet to a few ounces. The largest an indoor gardener would usually need would be ¾ cubic foot, which makes a package 12 x 12 x 9 inches. Peat moss comes compressed and will be much greater in volume when it is opened and fluffed up. When we refer to a "part" or "portion" of peat moss, we mean in its loosened state. If it is very dry, sprinkle it with a little hot water and let it stand a few minutes for easier handling.

If you run across a label that says "sphagnum moss" or "long-fibered sphagnum moss," this means it is for a different use so don't buy it. In a pinch you can use vermiculite as a substitute for peat moss. Vermiculite is a heat-processed mica which consists of very small particles that tend to break down in the soil, so its benefits are limited in time.

Perlite is a lightweight, expanded volcanic rock that allows air to enter the soil for proper root development and also improves the drainage ability of the soil mix. It is a very important additive, but many people object to its whiteness. To change this, simply pour 2 tablespoons of Kitchen Bouquet meat flavoring and ¼ cup of water into a bowl and add 2 cups of perlite. Stir well and you have brown perlite. Or use food coloring. Mix 2 teaspoons red, ½ teaspoon yellow, and 1 teaspoon blue with ¼ cup of water and 2 cups of perlite. Perlite should not be tinted with food coloring until you are ready to use it as it will lighten if allowed to dry out.

Perlite

Sand must be "sharp sand" or "builder's sand." Do not use seashore sand because it is loaded with salt, but lake sand is all right. Sand is used in a desert-soil mix and can also be a substitute for perlite, although it does not provide as much aeration. It is sometimes used for decorative purposes on the planting surface. It can be bought in small bags or sometimes even by the pot.

Sand

Humus or leaf mold can be used interchangeably. Both are decomposed vegetable matter that provide organic nutrients. Humus is in a finer, more decomposed state than leaf mold, but they both have the same source. They are used in woodland and desert mixes.

Limestone reduces the acidity of your mix, to "sweeten the soil." A pinch per cup of mix is optional in the tropical, not needed in the woodland, and strongly advised for the desert mix.

Bone meal provides nutrients, which are released slowly over a period of time. The most important is phosphorus, which promotes root growth. This is used only in the desert mix.

Fertilizers are a no-no. The recipes we advise contain sufficient nutrients to keep your plants healthy, and rampant growth is not desired in a terrarium. There are some occasions when fertilizers are used, but not in the initial plantings, so they will be covered in the chapter on maintenance. In general you can forget about them in terrariums.

"Terrarium soil mixes" are now prepackaged and are widely available, but do not list their ingredients. Some are soilless mixtures, others have varying ratios of the ingredients we have discussed. We prefer to mix our own growing medium, because we know exactly what's in it and can make adjustments for the individual environments. We certainly can't advise you against these mixes, but remember that you are paying for the mixing and packaging. If you do use one, try to decide if it seems a little heavy. Perlite or sand can be used to lighten the mix. We have had excellent results with the Swiss Farms mix, although we do lighten it a bit with perlite. For woodland environments the addition of humus is very important. Desert terrariums should not be planted with a general-purpose terrarium mix.

Making a soil mix is like
making a cake batter

Preparing Your Soil Mix

Mixing soil is like mixing a cake batter. Assemble your ingredients, follow your recipe, measure the correct proportions into a bowl, and stir well. If you are planning to make future terrariums (and we hope you are), make large batches and store them. Be sure to label each mix, since over a period of time it is easy to forget just what you have stirred up.

If your mix is dusty, sprinkle on a little water. You want a barely moist mixture, and dust indicates that some moisture is needed.

Tropical Soil Mix

3 parts sterilized potting soil

2 parts perlite or sand

1 part peat moss or vermiculite

1 pinch limestone per cup of mix (optional)

Woodland Soil Mix

3 parts sterilized potting soil

2 parts perlite or sand

1 part peat moss or vermiculite

1 part leaf mold or humus

Desert Soil Mix

1 part sterilized potting soil	or 2 parts packaged cactus (sandy) soil
½ part leaf mold or humus	1 part perlite
1 part sand	1 part leaf mold or humus

1 pinch limestone per cup of mix

1 pinch bonemeal per cup of mix

These three soil mixes will be referred to throughout this book, so we suggest you put a mark at this place in the book. We will usually say "add three cups of woodland soil mix" or "add desert soil mix" rather than giving the recipe. Then you can refer to the page for the ingredients and proportions, or type them on recipe cards.

5 Choosing Plants for Your Terrarium

Plants, of course, are what a terrarium is all about. Terrarium conditions are ideal for some plants, good for others, and unacceptable for still others. There are dozens of plants that can be grown in terrariums if you are careful to accommodate their special needs. We recommend those we have found to be the most foolproof, widely available, and attractive. They are arranged by terrarium environment and are listed by their common names, with the botanical names following.

Plant shopping is always enjoyable, so allow plenty of time to make your choices. Since you may also be picking up other items for your terrarium, look for the best-stocked source you can find. Garden centers and nurseries that also handle indoor plants usually have the widest selections. Stores that specialize in plants, as opposed to cut flowers, are generally excellent and often have special terrarium plant sections. You may find plants for the tropical and desert environments in a variety store or even a supermarket, but there you are likely to be entirely on your own, since informed plant salesmen are very rare.

Pick your plants carefully. The most important considerations are the environment, size, and the overall effect you want to achieve. But you must also learn how to pick a healthy plant. Choose a reputable store that carries a wide selection of plants. Don't look for bargains; you need only a few plants and should look for the best ones, not the cheapest. You can

Choosing healthy plants is vital for successful terrariums

tell a lot about a plant just by looking at it. Leaves that show signs of yellowing, brown spots, or drooping should never be purchased. Check the bottoms of leaves, growing tips, and the stems for insects. In general, the more compact and bushy a plant is, the better it will do; avoid spindly or elongated ones.

Don't compromise on a second-rate plant because you are eager to plant a terrarium. It's better to visit another store to see what else is around. It's also a good idea to drop in on your favorite source every so often to check on what's available. Plant stock can vary widely from time to time, and you will find all kinds of surprises every time you visit.

Be sure to assemble all of the plants you have chosen for one terrarium before you complete your purchase. When you see them in a group you may decide to make substitutions to improve your design.

Tropical Environment Plants

These plants form the basis for most popular house plant collections because they can tolerate the warm, dry atmosphere produced by modern heating methods. They will be much happier in the warm, *moist* atmosphere of your terrarium. They are especially recommended for beginning and intermediate projects, decorative and narrow-neck containers, and warmer locales.

Arrowhead. *Syngonium.* Comes in several varieties; any of the small plants will do. Extremely hardy, with solid green or variegated leaves shaped like arrowheads. Stem cuttings root easily in well-moistened perlite or sand. Good grower, so allow enough room.

Baby's Tears. *Helxine soleirolii.* Marvelous, tiny-leaved ground cover. Best in foreground. Stays low, spreads well. Can be separated into two plants from one pot. Can't take an overly moist terrarium. If they grow tall, clip tops back and new leaves will start.

Arrowhead,
Baby's Tears

Above: Boxwood, Chinese Evergreen, Coral Berry. *Left:* Creeping Fig, Dracaena

Boxwood. *Buxus.* Excellent subject with small shiny green leaves. Slow growing, bushy, can be pruned to hold shape. Tolerates low light.

Chinese Evergreen. *Aglaonema.* Super tough, slow growing, tolerates low light. Large, lance-shaped leaves. Can get tall, so provide for height.

Coral Berry. *Ardisia crispa.* Bushy, slow-growing plant with large shiny leaves. As a house plant it has clusters of red berries, but it will probably be strictly a foliage plant in your terrarium.

Creeping Fig. *Ficus repens.* Hardy, spreading ground cover; best at front and sides. Small, heart-shaped leaves. Cuttings will root easily in a terrarium. May grow up container walls.

Dracaena. Of the many dracaenas used as house plants, *D. sanderiana* (left) with white-edged, sword shaped leaves and *D. godseffiana* (right) with shiny, white- or gold-dotted leaves are best for terrariums. *Sanderiana* may have several stems per pot and will look sparse if separated.

48

Above: Dwarf Japanese Sweet Flag, English Ivy, Euonymus. *Right:* Fittonia, Iresine

Dwarf Japanese Sweet Flag. *Acorus gramineus pusillus.* Very hardy, with grasslike leaves in a somewhat stiff, tufted or fan shape; 4 inches at maximum. Leaves often variegated white and green.

English Ivy. *Hedera helix.* Widely used outdoors and as a houseplant. Many varieties, but look for small or variegated leaves and small plants. Cuttings will root in moist perlite or sand. Excellent spreading ground cover. Likes bright light.

Euonymus. Very hardy, multi-branched plant with variegated leaves ranging from white to yellow. Forms upright bush shape.

Fittonia. Fine all-around plant. Often called mosaic plant for its patterned leaves, which come in red-veined and white-veined varieties. Upright when young, more creeping as it grows. Use small plants.

Iresine. Leaves range from reddish purple to yellow-green. Often called bloodleaf. Pick bushy plants and pinch back growing tips before planting to keep shape. Bright light gives best show of color.

49

Above: Maranta, Parlor Palm, Peperomia. *Left:* Philodendron, Pilea

Maranta. Large multi-colored leaves fold at night to give it the common name of prayer plant. Several varieties available; all small plants excellent. Bushy, so best for middle to back. Likes bright light. Its cousin, the brightly colored peacock plant, *Calathea*, also fine.

Parlor Palm. *Chamaedorea*. Marvelous miniature palm, also known as *Neanthe bella*. Very hardy, slow grower, and tolerant of low light. One of the best all-around terrarium plants. Give it adequate headroom.

Peperomia. Large family of easily grown, popular house plants. All small ones are fine, especially the emerald ripple, *P. caperata*, and the watermelon, *P. sandersii*. Good growers. Stick a leaf with a bit of stem halfway into the soil mix to form new plants.

Philodendron. Probably the most popular and easiest grown house plant around. Pick small plants and small-leafed varieties. May need pruning, but generally excellent ground cover or small plant.

Pilea. Many species that often look unrelated. Best are aluminum, *P. cadierei*, with silver-blotched leaves; artillery, *P. microphylla*, with tiny leaves; creeping, *P. depressa*, for ground cover, and "Moon Valley." Small sections of the creeping variety will root easily.

50

Above: Podocarpus, Pothos, Sansevieria. *Right:* Spathiphyllum, Strawberry Begonia

Podocarpus. Very hardy and tolerant plant; will take form of a tree. Can be pruned to hold shape. Use in middle or back for height. Best in bright light, but can adapt to less.

Pothos. *Scindapsus.* Sometimes called devil's ivy. Looks like a relative of philodendron and is equally hardy. Heart-shaped, white-flecked leaves, markings more pronounced in bright light.

Sansevieria. Be *very* careful to buy the low-growing "Hahnii." Do *not* get the tall-growing relative known as snake plant or mother-in-law's tongue. Extremely hardy, slow-growing, tolerant of low light.

Spathiphyllum. An airy-looking plant with dark green, lance-shaped leaves growing from a main stem. May bear leaf-shaped flowers called spathes, which resemble the blossoms of calla lilies. Tolerates low light. Recommended variety is "Clevelandii."

Strawberry Begonia. *Saxifraga sarmentosa.* Also known as mother-of-thousands and strawberry geranium. Perfect ground cover with round, hairy leaves. Puts out runners which form new plants at the ends.

51

Woodland Environment Plants

Most of the plants for this environment come from the floors of cool woodland and forest areas. In your terrarium they will create a naturalistic section of nature where pine cones, fallen leaves, and moss complement the textures and shapes of the plants. Ferns are predominant, and terrariums provide by far the best way to raise small ferns in the home, since internal humidity eliminates the daily misting many require. All prefer low temperatures, and high ones (above 75°) are not conducive to growth. They particularly like cool nights.

Asparagus Fern. *Asparagus plumosus.* Not a fern, but has fernlike appearance. Likes bright light. Can be bushy, but is usually treelike. Excellent for height. Be sure to get *plumosus*, not any other asparagus varieties.

Mimosa. *Mimosa pudica.* Leaves fold up at the slightest touch, hence commonly called sensitive plant. Rather treelike, light and graceful. Good for middle or background. Will rapidly unfold after planting, but don't overhandle.

Asparagus Fern,
Mimosa

Above: Norfolk Island Pine, Partridgeberry, Pellionia. *Right:* Pipsissewa, Rattlesnake Plantain

Norfolk Island Pine. *Araucaria.* Lends grace and height, especially good in large containers. Look for smaller plants, and snip off tops to keep compact. Best as tree form in background.

Partridgeberry. *Mitchella repens.* Dependable plant with dark green, oval leaves and red berries. Found throughout northeast woods. Roots easily and stays low. Can be ordered by mail if not found in stores.

Pellionia. Excellent creeping ground cover. Most commonly found varieties are *P. pulchra* and *P. daveauana.* Oval leaves, pinkish stems.

Pipsissewa. *Chimaphila.* Low-growing plant with clusters of leathery leaves. Both spotted wintergreen, *C. maculata,* and common pipsissewa, *C. umbellata,* will thrive. Easily shipped by mail.

Rattlesnake Plantain. *Goodyera pubescens.* A woodland orchid which may even bloom. Rosette of oval-shaped leaves with white variations. Fine foreground or accent plant. Can be ordered by mail if not available locally.

53

Members of the huge fern family are the basis for most woodland terrariums

Ferns

These are the stars of the woodland terrarium. Small specimens will thrive in your closed containers. Some of the best and most readily available are covered here. Others are also available and you should not be limited by this list. Allow room for all ferns to grow and prosper as new fronds often start appearing a few weeks after planting. They vary widely in texture and appearance, many not fitting into the usual "fern" look.

Bird's-nest Fern. *Asplenium nidus*. Best known of the many spleenworts. Dependable terrarium plant. Long, smooth fronds, more leaflike than ferny. New fronds unroll from the center and turn bright green. Other small spleenworts, such as ebony spleenwort, *A. Platyneuron*, also fine.

Cliffbrake Fern. *Pellaea rotundifolia*. Not at all fernlike in appearance. Long stems spaced with dark green, button-shaped fronds give rise to the nickname of button fern. Good ground cover, or foreground plant. Stays low and very striking.

Fluffy Ruffles Fern. Low-growing with very finely divided fronds to make an almost solid bush. This and other small growing varieties of *Nephrolepis exaltata*, such as "Whitmanii" and mini-ruffles, are fine. It's a relative of the popular Boston fern, which is too large for terrarium use.

Above: Bird's-nest Fern
Below: Cliffbrake Fern, Fluffy Ruffles Fern

Maidenhair Fern,
Rabbit's-foot Fern,
Table Fern

Holly Fern. *Cyrtomium*. Tolerant of temperature changes and low light. Several varieties may be found; all are hardy terrarium plants. Tends to have stiff stems and fronds resembling holly leaves. Look for small plants.

Maidenhair Fern. *Adiantum*. Beautiful, light effect from lacy fronds held erect on dark stems. Many varieties; all small ones good. Some fronds may brown naturally and need pruning.

Polypody. *Polypodium*. Large family; for terrariums, hare's-foot fern, *P. aureum*, and common, *P. vulgare*, are best. Grows from a creeping brown stem, very hardy.

Rabbit's-foot Fern. *Davallia*. Grows from creeping rootstock with hairy scales. Fronds light and feathery, somewhat like carrot tops. Related deer's-foot, *D. canariensis*, and squirrel's-foot, *D. trichomanioides*, also fine.

Shield Fern. *Dryopteris*. Over 1000 species, most for outdoors. Wood fern, *D. marginalis*, and beech fern, *D. phegopteris*, are fine when small. Provide room as they are good growers.

Table Fern. *Pteris*. Rather large family and any small specimens will be fine. Hardy, dependable, with serrated, usually slightly ruffled leaves. Some have variegated fronds with tones of light green and silver.

Club Moss. *Lycopodium*. Actually a fern relative and not a true moss. Found in eastern and northwestern

56

woods. Small plants (4 to 6 inches) best; often used as background in medium-sized terrariums. Roots easily.

Selaginella. Related to the ferns, but looks like moss. Good ground cover, spreads rapidly, tolerates low light. Can be divided to get several plants from each pot. Small pieces root easily in a terrarium.

Mosses and Lichens

These two types of ground cover come in many, many varieties. Readily available in outdoor locations. Grow on rocks, logs, and moist earth. Inside, moss will do best if immediately put in a terrarium. May eventually die out, but still holds its form and looks well. Sometimes mosses, but rarely lichens, can be found in stores. Use in foregrounds for accents.

Moss can also be used for a banking or carpeting effect. Large pieces can be separated into smaller ones for use in many areas. Sheet moss which has been dried and artificially colored is not recommended. Live moss is sometimes used in terrariums as an outward-facing liner to make a pocket for the drainage and soil mix.

Club Moss,
Selaginella

Mosses and Lichens

Ball Cactus

Desert Environment Plants

Plants for the desert terrarium are divided into cacti and succulents. There are thousands of varieties of these plants, and we can only list a few of the most popular and readily found. The wonderful thing about these plants is that almost all can be given the same treatment. There are certain exceptions, of course, but in general cacti and succulents are extremely hardy and demand only bright light, preferably direct sun, and not too much water.

Although we show only a few of the varieties available, any plant you find that looks like one of our examples can safely be treated like the one pictured.

Cob Cactus

Cacti

Ball Cactus. *Notocactus*. Ball-shaped when young, later columnar. Clusters of very fine spines in vertical rows. Spines may be white or yellow. May flower if given good sun.

Cob Cactus. *Lobivia*. The Latin name is an anagram of Bolivia, where they were first found. Mostly columnar bodies, some globular. Many varieties and hybrids. Often ribbed, with sharp spines. Most small and slow-growing. Not fussy.

Above: Columnar Cactus, Easter Lily Cactus, Gherkin Cactus. *Right:* Grafted Cactus, Hedgehog Cactus

Columnar Cactus. *Cereus.* Once a very large genus, now reduced as many species have been moved to other categories. Mostly upright growing, with deep ribbing and many spines.

Easter Lily Cactus. *Echinopsis.* Also called sea urchin cactus. Generally globular, ribbed plants with tufts of spines. Many hybrids available. Very tolerant, always performs well.

Gherkin or Peanut Cactus. *Chamaecereus silvestri.* Popular, hardy, small cactus. Multiple columnlike growth pattern led to popular names. With a cool, dry winter, it may bloom in spring.

Grafted Cactus. Available in most stores under names such as moon cactus or bunny cactus. Tops are yellow, orange, red, or grotesquely formed and grafted on top of another cactus. Interesting novelty, but one per planting is sufficient.

Hedgehog or Barrel Cactus. *Echinocactus.* Extremely popular and varied group. Mostly globular or slightly cylindrical with ribs and spines. Well known is *E. grusoni*, with many ribs and arching spines. Among the easiest to grow.

59

Above: Old Man Cactus, Pincushion Cactus, Prickly Pear.
Left: Rebutia, Star Cactus

Old Man Cactus. *Cephalocereus senilis.* Best known member of this genus, it is covered with white or yellow "hair" which tends to hide needle-sharp spines, so don't be fooled by the soft look. Sure-fire performer. Other species also have "hair" and grow upright.

Pincushion or Powderpuff Cactus. *Mammillaria.* Probably the least demanding of the entire group, may even bloom. Mostly globular or slightly cylindrical. Nipplelike protuberances spiral around body, spines growing from tips. Many varieties, all recommended.

Prickly Pear. *Opuntia.* Very large group now found all over the world but originally from the Americas. Many forms; best known indoors are probably beaver-tail and bunny ears. No true spines, but tiny growths called glochidia are even meaner, so handle with care. Very hardy, and good grower.

Rebutia. Small globular cacti. Keep very dry and cool from October to January as buds form, then begin watering and you will often get flowers. Even if not, an excellent all-around cactus.

Star Cactus. *Astrophytum.* Small, globular plants, often with geometric patterns or pronounced ribbing. Few or no spines. Popular varieties are sand dollar and bishop's cap. Dependable and undemanding.

Above: Agave, Aloe, Crassula. *Right:* Echeveria, Euphorbia

Succulents

Agave. Rosette form, leaves often white-striped. Called century plant because it takes many years to bloom. Most are too large for indoor use, but very young, small ones are fine. Recommended are *A. victoriae-reginae*, *A. americana*, and *A. stricta*.

Aloe. Low-growing, rosette form. Leaves often shaded in green, gray, and white. Often confused with agave. Partridge-breasted, tiger, and lace all good choices. Slow grower.

Crassula. Very large genus of widely varying plants. Best known is the jade plant, *C. portulacea* or *C. argentea*. No easy way to tell its members are related. Other good choices are *C. lycopodioides* (shoe lace), *C. falcata*, *C. socialis*, and *C. lactea*.

Echeveria. Large genus, usually low, globular, with a rosette appearance. Leaves are thick, range from gray to green. May drop lower or outer leaves naturally. Often available in tiny specimens.

Euphorbia. Succulents that often look like cacti. Usually branched, sometimes grotesquely, and with spines. Best known is crown-of-thorns; the miniature version, *E. splendens prostata*, is fine. Very hardy, but smaller sizes sometimes not available.

Above: Gasteria, Haworthia, Kalanchoe. *Left:* Pachyphytum, Sedum

Gasteria. Excellent subject that stays small and is not particular. Fleshy leaves opposite each other, with white markings. Appearance and needs similar to aloe, but can get by without direct sun.

Haworthia. Relative of aloe and gasteria, with similar needs. Usually a rosette form with no stem. Leaves often marked with white. Generally compact, but some are columnar. *H. cymbiformis* and *H. fasciata* are two of the best.

Kalanchoe. Widely varying genus, with many plants more leafed than most succulents. Usually small, upright grower. Panda plant, *K. tomentosa*, is excellent; all small ones are fine. *K. blossfeldiana*, sold in florist's shops for red-orange bloom, is good if found small. Water all year; no dry period needed.

Pachyphytum. Large genus, usually low-growing thick-leaved, with rosette appearance. Similar in looks and needs to echeveria. Slow-growing, compact, good all around plant.

Sedum. Well known in outdoor rock gardens as stonecrop; many suitable for indoor use. Some spread, others bushy and upright. Any small ones are fine.

62

Sempervivum. Practically indestructible small plants with dense rosette of leaves. Hen-and-chicks has smaller plants around edge. Also called houseleek and live-for-ever. All varieties good.

Sempervivum

Cacti and succulents combined in a desert environment

Planting Procedures
and Maintenance

Soil Mix

Soil Separator

Drainage

Charcoal

These are the elements needed for a simple, first-time terrarium

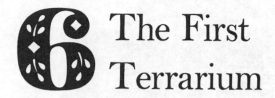

The First Terrarium

If you have read chapters one through five — and only if so — you are now ready to build an absolutely foolproof, guaranteed-successful, first-time terrarium. It will be easy, fun, and quick. Though simple, it incorporates all of the steps for building larger, more advanced terrariums and provides you with a basic foundation for all future plantings.

If you haven't already done so, pick the location for your first terrarium. The plants will come from the tropical list, so any bright or medium-light location is fine. That means good reading light during most of the day but no direct sun. We are presuming that for this first-time (or review) terrarium you have no materials on hand. Everything you will need is easily found. The best place to start is a good garden center or a large plant store. If you don't find everything there, a department store and what was once called your "local five and dime" should have the others.

Be sure that the container for your first terrarium has an opening large enough to permit you to reach inside. Later you will be able to work with containers that have smaller openings, but don't try it on your first planting. Look for a medium-sized brandy snifter or a decorative food storage or apothecary jar. On your pantry shelf you might find a gallon food jar or a wide-mouthed refrigerator storage jar. Cover any bright colors or wording on the lid with dark green or brown paint.

Three first-time terrariums, made from the instructions in this chapter by people who had never built a terarrium before

A terrarium of this size will take two or possibly three plants, plus a low-growing ground-cover plant or moss. Buy them in 2-inch pots or smaller. If the plants we suggest aren't available in small pots, any of the tropical plants listed in chapter five will work. When you shop, look for a medium-sized plant, a small plant (or two), and one ground cover. As in a Chinese restaurant, pick one from Column A, one from Column B, and one from Column C.

A	B	C
Medium (3 to 4 inches)	*Small (2 to 3 inches)*	*Ground cover*
Chinese Evergreen	Iresine (Bloodleaf)	Baby's Tears
Boxwood	Euonymus	Philodendron
Maranta	Pilea	Creeping Pilea
Parlor Palm	Coral Berry	Moss

These plants come in many sizes and shapes, so try the ones you like in a combination before making a final choice. Really hunt for small plants, because when it is time to do the planting, you will discover the container is smaller than you imagined.

A Terrarium Shopping List

Now it's time to go on a shopping trip. We've made out a list of everything you need. If you already have some of the items on hand, just strike them off the list.

Cleaning materials — glass cleaner or detergent, paper towels

Container — one you can get your hand in, about 2- or 3-quart size

Gravel — two or three handfuls for drainage

Charcoal — small package of horticultural grade

Soil separator — fiber glass or other synthetic material

Sterilized potting soil — one-pound bag

Peat moss — small package

Soil lightener — ½ cup sand or small bag perlite

Plants — discussed above

Sprayer — bulb sprayer, plant mister, or empty spray-type glass-cleaner bottle

Tools — blunt instrument for tamping (cork on an ice pick), soil placer (iced-tea or serving spoon), scissors, measuring cup, mixing bowl

Natural decorative elements — easily found in yards, wooded areas, or vacant lots. Use larger pebbles, small rocks, small pine cones, or other elements from the ground. If you use organic elements, bake them in a 250° oven for two hours to avoid mold. No plastic ducks or wishing wells!

A suggested design for a first terrarium

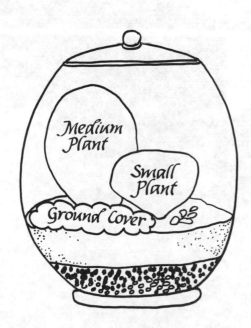

Planting Procedure

Once you have all of the elements on hand you are ready to plant. Choose a time when you can work for up to an hour without interruption. Find a smooth, well-lighted work space which allows you plenty of room to spread out; put down a layer of newspaper to ease the clean-up. Before you begin, read through the entire procedure so you know what's coming next. Relax and have fun; no one is going to give you a grade.

1. Clean the container thoroughly inside and out. Rinse well if you use a detergent. Dry it with paper towels or a lint-free cloth. Assemble everything on the work surface.

2. Place about ¾ inch of gravel in the bottom of the container. Sprinkle 1 tablespoon of charcoal over it.

3. Cut your soil separator and then rest it on the drainage, barely reaching the sides of the container. Stay on the large side for the first cut and then trim it down.

4. Prepare 3 cups of tropical soil mix:

1½ cups sterilized potting soil
1 cup perlite or sand
½ cup peat moss or vermiculite

Stir well and spoon in a layer about 1 inch deep on top of the soil separator. More will be added later.

5. Decide approximately how you want your plants arranged. Don't just start by sticking a plant any old place. Leave the plants in their pots and place them on the work surface in an attractive grouping, as shown in the middle photograph.

6. Use your spoon to dig a hole right down to the soil separator where the largest plant is to go. Remove the plant from its pot by placing your index and middle finger on either side of the stem, turning the pot upside down, and whacking the bottom with the bowl of your spoon, or the palm of your hand. An alternate method is to bang the edge of the pot on a corner of a table or counter top until it falls out. Put the plant into the hole and see how it looks. It will probably sit too high, so take the plant out of the terrarium and gently crumble some soil away from the bottom with your fingers. You can do this onto the paper, or into your soil mix. Replace the plant. With your spoon, scoop some soil mix around it to hold it in place, tamping it if necessary.

7. Following the same procedure, dig a hole for the second plant and place it in position. If you have a third plant, do the same. Then fill in with soil mix to the desired level, which should be even with the surface the plants had in their pots. Use your tamper or fingers to press down the surface firmly. Add more soil mix if you need it and retamp.

71

8. Position your ground cover. If it is potted, dig a small hole. Moss requires only a slight depression. Use your fingers or tamper to pack soil firmly after planting. Use sterilized potting soil as a top dressing if you don't like the appearance of perlite.

Now place your decorative surface elements. Move them around until they have a natural, casual look. Bury any larger elements slightly to give a "settled in" appearance. Three or four small pebbles in a group are more interesting than the same number scattered about.

9. When your terrarium has achieved a natural look, give it a combination watering and cleaning with one of the watering devices from the shopping list. It's important that you don't overwater and it's better to stay on the dry side. About ¼ cup should be plenty. Begin spraying at the top and wash down the sides if needed. Clean off the plants also. You can prevent water spots by wiping off excess water with a piece of paper towel wrapped around the spoon handle or your finger. Clean the outside of the container, but be careful not to get any glass cleaner inside.

10. Cover the terrarium, place it in its new home, and start watching to see how well the moisture cycle has been established. Either the amount of water you have put in is just right (rah!), not enough (easily corrected),

or too much (a problem, but can be remedied). To determine this, check the terrarium at least daily to determine how much misting occurs and the color of the soil mix.

The completed terrarium

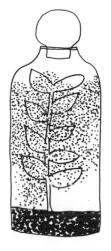

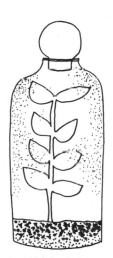

Heavy mist at all times, soil mix very dark.
Too much water. Leave cover half open for a day, replace, and check next day. Continue this procedure until light mist forms daily and soil mix color lightens.

Light mist daily, soil mix medium dark.
Just right, don't touch anything.

No misting at all, soil mix light.
Not enough water. Add one teaspoon of water every third day until light mist forms daily and soil mix darkens.

When you have properly balanced the moisture level you have truly completed your first terrarium. To insure good health, give it a fifteen-minute airing every week or two. This isn't essential, but is an excellent way to prevent mildew, and also gives the plants a change of air. Opening it for this short amount of time will not upset the moisture balance.

Intermediate Terrariums— Onward and Upward

Once you have planted your first successful terrarium, you will be eager to move on to other projects. All of the steps and principles you used can be applied to a wide range of plantings to extend your terrarium experience; with each you will become more proficient and design conscious. Now is the time to begin experimenting with different plants, containers, and arrangements.

For the next few terrariums, try to stick with containers that have openings large enough to let you reach inside, but begin working with simple tools. This experience will prepare you for smaller-necked containers, which must be planted mainly with the aid of tools, and eventually for narrow-neck bottles. Some useful tools are a large wooden spoon, a tamper made from a cork on a fondu fork or ice pick, and a long artist's brush. Giant wooden tweezers, called terrarium tongs, are very helpful; the wrong end makes an excellent tamping tool.

Let your imagination run free, and experiment with any container you like in the one-quart to two-gallon size. Don't be in a hurry to take on a five-gallon aquarium or giant brandy snifter until you have put together a few medium-sized terrariums. You'll discover that you learn more about plants, procedures, and your own design ideas with every project. It's usually best to use tropical plants for your first few intermediate projects; then move to the woodland environment as you choose larger containers.

A cut bottle and a miniature terrarium,
both excellent for intermediate terrarium builders

Three intermediate terrariums easily assembled
by anyone with a bit of experience

Remember to change your soil-mix recipe for the woodland planting.

This is a good time to broaden your use of natural decorative elements. Take a walk through a nearby wooded area, a vacant lot, or even your back yard. If you go to a park, take only nonliving material from the ground, and only what you will use soon. The natural appearance of the park should be left undisturbed by your visit. In woods and vacant lots you can take bits of moss and lichen, for nature is constantly at work and will soon replace them if you select areas where the material is plentiful. Use these collecting trips to gain ideas about how natural landscapes look so you can re-create them in your terrariums.

Any organic matter that might develop mold or mildew, such as branches and twigs, should be placed in a 250° oven for two hours for sterilizing.

Here are some of the best natural elements:

Small sections of fallen tree limbs, branches, or twigs. Don't break
anything off a living tree.

Seed pods, acorns, dried flower heads, and pine cones.

Well-dried leaves, preferably on the tough, leathery side, like rhodo-
dendron or eucalyptus, and evergreen needles.

Pebbles and rocks, in a variety of sizes, colors, and textures. Seashore
pebbles can also be used; wash them well to remove salt deposits.

Moss, found in many locations and many forms. Collect only what
you plan to use immediately as it is hard to keep moss alive outside
of a terrarium. Lichen, often found growing on rocks and tree
bark, is fine for woodland terrariums.

Banking materials, such as flat rocks or bark from a fallen tree.

Some natural elements can also be purchased. Look for rocks, gravel,
and sand at tropical fish stores or garden centers. Plant stores sometimes
sell wood chips or redwood bark in small quantities. Moss can occasionally be found in stores that stock terrarium plants.

This beautiful mushroom-shaped terrarium by Christen has a hand-blown top,
ceramic base, and allows a graceful spreading of foliage

A woodland planting inside one of
a line of leaded glass terrariums made
by New Renaissance Glass Works.
All echo the feeling of Victorian
"Wardian Cases"

This is a good time to try the perlite-coloring process if you didn't use
it for your first terrarium. The white perlite is easily turned dark by the
use of meat flavoring or food coloring, as described in the soil-mix chapter. If you are doing several terrariums over a period of time, mix up a
batch with meat flavoring to have on hand. Perlite dyed with food coloring must be used right away as it loses color when stored.

New England Partridgeberry Bowls

With a little advance planning, you can easily assemble a dozen traditional partridgeberry bowls for Christmas gifts in one evening. The
advance planning is needed because the plants for this terrarium are
somewhat difficult to find in stores, but they may be easily procured by
mail. (See mail sources at end of book.) The early New England containers were hand-blown crystal bowls, but you can use any small
decorative glass container that has a lid, such as an apothecary jar, globe,
or large goblet. In addition to partridgeberry and mosses, these containers may also hold pipsissewa and rattlesnake plantain. The bowl
should be *very* full of plants to create the best effect.

If you want to line the bottom of the bowl with live moss, sphagnum moss, or any other moss put the green side out. Then into this "nest," or into the bottom of the unlined container, place a few tablespoons of gravel, sprinkled with charcoal. You may even use charcoal alone for the drainage layer if you prefer. Mix two parts of potting soil with one part of peat moss and lay down a ¾-inch layer of this mix. Some bowls are planted in sphagnum moss only, but the addition of soil mix will lengthen the life span of your bowl. Add the plants, making sure they are well tamped into the soil mix. Plants sold by mail usually come with bare roots, but easily settle into their new environment. Then add the mosses to create a very lush, even crowded effect. The partridgeberry, with its bright red accents, should be the most visible element of this planting. Unrooted pieces of partridgeberry will take root in either moss or soil mix.

Give the planting a *very* light sprinkling of water, add the lid, and place it in bright light in the coolest location you have. Although the closed terrarium environment makes it possible to keep these hardy outdoor plants alive and healthy in the house, they do better away from excessive heat. Follow the rules for watering or ventilating set forth in the preceding chapter.

Prepare the bowls at least ten days before you present them, so that you can establish a proper moisture balance, and include a note describing how to care for the bowl. You can be sure your gift will be among the most memorable and personal of the year.

The New England partridgeberry bowl, a traditional
yuletide decoration you can make in minutes

A gift terrarium should include a note describing possible locations and a misting guide. Use a shopping bag stuffed with paper to prevent tipping

Hanging Terrariums

Hanging terrariums are a dramatic way to display your skill. If you hang them near a window, these terrariums also have the advantage of ideal light. All three environments can be built in hanging containers, but remember that the desert plants need sun or very bright light and no top. Use a container that has a rounded bottom for the best effect. Square containers or those with any kind of base generally look awkward when they are hanging.

If you plan to hang your terrarium from the ceiling, check the construction material first. You may be lucky and have an exposed beam or be able to drill through the ceiling and hit one. A plasterboard or plaster ceiling will require an expanding toggle bolt or a "molly" anchor bolt. Check with your superintendent if you live in an apartment or inquire at a hardware store for the proper method and needed items. An easier method is to use a wall bracket set in the side of a window frame or a simple screw-in hook from the top of the frame. Hangers can be found in plant stores; better yet, make them from cord, leather, or macramé. For a sensational floating look, use a nylon hanger, which can also be purchased or easily assembled from nylon fishing line. This tends to be invisible, especially at night, and makes your terrarium appear to be suspended in midair.

Whatever method you use, weight is an important consideration. The small hanging terrarium in the photograph weighs 10 pounds; larger ones could weigh 20 pounds or more. Make sure your hook, hanger, and method of securing the hook can support your project. We don't want any beautiful terrariums going crash in the night.

Planting procedures for hanging woodland and tropical terrariums are exactly the same as for standing ones. Desert instructions are covered in the next chapter. To hold the container steady while you plant it, place a small terry-cloth towel across the top of a saucepan or casserole and place your container in this support. This is especially important for a desert terrarium in a plastic container as it scratches easily.

Although you should select the spot where your container is to be placed before building it, we prefer putting the hook in place after the terrarium is built. Then you can make a minor change in position if you want. These terrariums are best when viewed slightly below eye level, and should be in a spot where no one will accidentally bonk his head.

A hanging terrarium appears to float when supported by nylon fishline

When planting a round-bottomed hanging terrarium, use a towel in a casserole or heavy pot to make a nest

Miniature terrariums can
perk up locations too small
for other sizes

Miniature Terrariums

Although most people like to work into larger sizes as they advance in terrarium projects, some prefer to make miniatures in containers of one-pint capacity or less. Whether you choose a food jar or one of the many decorative containers that are readily available and quite inexpensive, miniatures make perfect gifts, suitable for end tables, night stands, and similar spots where a small accent will look best.

Select your plants carefully. Look for tiny specimens and avoid rampant growers that climb right up the walls in the terrarium atmosphere.

Obviously, very small amounts of everything are needed; you can let the charcoal double as drainage material if your container is extremely small. Planting procedures are the same as for your first terrarium. You will find a teaspoon for placing soil mix and an ordinary wooden pencil for tamping are handy tools. Moss is probably the best surface cover, and one plant plus moss may be all you have room for in some containers. Decorative surface elements must be very small, and are often not needed; a few light-colored pieces of gravel or some sand can be used. Be extra careful of overwatering in these tiny containers because there is so little space where the excess can collect.

A particularly enjoyable way to work with these containers is to do three or four at one time, since little material is needed and the planting doesn't take much time. Then you can have a couple for yourself and others for gifts. They will be especially appreciated by anyone who likes plants but can't find the time to take care of them.

Use terrariums to brighten up an office desk

8 The Wonderful World of Cacti and Succulents

Your feelings about the incredibly large family of plants known as cacti and succulents is probably like your reaction to snails for dinner — you either love 'em or hate 'em. We are emphatically in the love 'em group. These marvelously varied and hardy plants create a miniature desert scene in a sunny window, where a woodland or tropical terrarium would bake. Since their containers cannot have lids, we call them topless terrariums. A desert terrarium needs very little water and is easy to maintain. The assembly steps are the same as for other terrariums, except that the moisture cycle is not established.

First let's distinguish between the words "cactus" and "succulent," because they can be confusing. There are many branches of the plant category known as succulents, and the cactus family is just one — the best known. Technically cacti are just one kind of succulent, but when you go into a plant store and ask to see succulents you will not be led to the cacti section. Since popular usage treats cacti as one group of plants and succulents as another, so will we.

The word succulent comes from the Latin *succus*, which means juice; many of the plants in this category have a juicy or fleshy quality. As a rule, the cacti you will use have no leaves; they have thick bodies that are globular or columnar, but sometimes branching or flat. Most have spines. Indoor succulents, on the other hand, usually have thick leaves or a leaf-

85

Desert terrariums and cats
enjoy warm sunny days

like structure, often in a compact rosette or circular arrangement. Both cacti and succulents come from arid and semi-arid regions of the world and have the ability either to store water in their bodies or to exist for long periods of time without it. In your home they can go for days without watering, and for many a dry rest period is essential.

One reason we like desert terrariums is that grouped plants are vastly more interesting than single specimens. People who are bored by a cactus in a pot get a whole new perspective from a group of desert plants in a natural scene. We think this planting form will become much more widespread as good examples become available, and we hope yours will be an inspiration to others. An extra enjoyment from desert terrariums is the use of different colors to represent layers of soil. This looks difficult, but is simple once you know the secret, and you soon will.

Containers for your desert scene duplicate many of those used for woodland and tropical terrariums, but without the tops. This applies to glass globes, brandy snifters, fishbowls, and other decorative containers. You might also use a soufflé or other baking dish. Small-neck containers are not advisable; topless terrariums call for an open, broad look. An excellent choice is a simple rectangular container, such as an aquarium. Many aquariums have a top frame that can be removed for a desert scene, since it is only needed to support a cover.

Cut bottles of all kinds make excellent topless terrariums, especially those in the one-gallon size. They do not need to be transparent, since the

These six plants are vastly more interesting turned into a miniature desert

top is not replaced and you will probably bring the surface up to a level just below the cut edge. You may also want to construct a glass rectangle for a special location.

Plastic, which is not suitable for a closed terrarium, works beautifully for a desert container. Its light weight, wide availability, and varied styles make it a fine choice.

Plants for the desert terrarium are easily found; you will discover more suitable desert varieties than for either of the other environments. Unless you go in for large or rare specimens, you can safely pick any cactus or succulent from a plant store, garden center, or even a variety store and be assured that its needs will be very similar to those of the others you choose.

"Can a little cactus from the American Southwest find true happiness with a sturdy succulent from Africa?" you may ask. Yes! Succulents like a bit more water than cacti and not such a dry winter but in general they aren't fussy and you can plant them together. The watering procedure for a topless terrarium enables you to take care of any special plant needs. An all-cactus, all-succulent, or mixed group will work well.

Most small cactus and succulent plants are quite inexpensive. Shop for a range of sizes, shapes, and textures. This is easy, since even two plants of the same species can vary in appearance. Tiny, tiny specimens are perfect for tucking into unusual spots, especially at the base of larger ones.

Desert plants should not be crowded in the new setting. In nature they often grow some distance apart. Leave room for some bare surface and some natural decorative elements. There is no real ground-cover plant for desert terrariums as there is for woodland and tropical. Sedum comes the closest, but bare ground is part of the natural desert look. Dish gardens are often made in small shallow containers, and a massed effect works fine for this size. We much prefer larger containers and more spacing to create a natural effect.

It's impossible to tell you how many plants you will need, but as a rough guide, a 12-inch sphere will take eight or nine plants, none taller than 5 inches. A five-gallon aquarium (16 x 8 x 10 inches) can use one large (5 to 6 inches), three medium (2 to 4 inches), and at least four small (1 to 2 inches) plants. These estimates allow room for rocks, dried wood, and other surface elements without crowding. As always in plant selection, assemble your plants before buying and let your eye be the final judge.

Handling prickly cactus plants takes a little luck or the proper tool, maybe both. There are three possible ways to do this. The first — to be able to pick them up, handle them, and replant them without getting spiked — may be the easiest. Some people have the knack and others don't. It isn't something you can learn except by handling lots of plants to discover their characteristics. If you have this talent, use it.

A layered cactus garden
is made by using different
tones of earth and sand

Several hundred cacti in
a store window; none are
over 1½ inches tall

If you don't, wear a pair of leather gloves (or one). A single one really works better as you still have a "regular" hand. Cloth or knitted gloves will snag on the spines. Leather protects your hands and at the same time gives you the freedom to handle cacti as you do other plants.

Method three is to use a "cactus handler." This can be a pair of ice tongs, a bacon turner, a hinged salad server, or a newspaper rolled up and folded to become a pair of giant tweezers. If you use any of these, be careful not to crush the plant or break the skin.

If you wear gloves you can remove cactus plants from their pots in the regular way, making a V with your middle and index fingers, putting it around the stem, and whacking the bottom of the pot. Another way to get the plant out of its pot is to put the eraser end of a pencil through the drainage hole and push upward. When the plant is loose, grasp it with your cactus handler or your hand. This works well with most cacti and succulents because the soil is very dry.

One final reminder. A desert terrarium cannot exist on less than bright light, and it should have direct sun for at least part of the day. If you can't provide a sunny location, or a spot near a sunny window, you should not choose this environment.

A Desert Terrarium Shopping List

Here's a shopping list to make sure you have everything you need, incorporating the special requirements of desert conditions.

Cleaning materials — glass or plastic cleaner, paper towels

Container, without a top

Gravel for drainage — buff, tan, or gray work best

Charcoal — a small bag

Soil separator — fiber glass or other synthetic material

A custom-made plastic desert planter intended for a sunny window ledge

Soil-mix ingredients — from chapter 4

Plants — discussed above

Tools — spoon, tamper, scissors, watercolor brush, and a "cactus handler" or leather gloves

Natural decorative elements — anything that might be found on the
surface of an arid or semi-arid region. These must be collected, so
keep your eye open for bare branches, rocks, thistles, seed pods.
Sand makes a good top dressing

Bulb sprayer — essential for initial and future watering because it
allows you to control the amount of water and where it goes

a. A desert soil mix is placed over the drainage, charcoal, and soil separator
b. Plants are positioned on an outline of the container to create the most dramatic effect

Planting the Desert Terrarium

Although the step-by-step procedures for the desert terrarium are very similar to those we have described before, there are important differences. These are covered in the individual steps, so be sure to read through all the instructions before starting. If you plan to use colored layers of sand, read the instructions for constructing the layers at the end of the chapter and follow them as part of step 4.

1. Clean the container, using a special plastic cleaner if you are using that material. Assemble all elements on a work space covered with newspapers.

2. Place a layer of drainage in the bottom of the container. The depth should be from ½ inch in small containers up to 1½ inches for a large aquarium. Add charcoal at the rate of one tablespoon per cup of drainage.

3. Cut the soil separator to fit on top of the drainage and just reach the edge of the container. Lay it in position. If you are using colored layers, read the instructions on page 96 at this point.

4. Prepare your soil mix, according to one of the desert recipes in chapter 4. Desert plants can live in a shallower layer of soil mix than other plants. A small desert terrarium should have a minimum of 1½ inches of soil-mix layer; in larger containers use 2½ inches. Place your mix in the container to about two-thirds the final depth.

5. Plan the positions of major banking, dry "rivers," and large rocks.

c. A leather glove makes handling a prickly cactus easy
d. Watering is done with a bulb mister

Leave the plants in their pots and arrange them with the natural surface elements on the work surface. Keep a random grouping with varying spaces between plants.

6. Dig a hole where the largest plant is to go. Remove the plant from its pot, using gloves or a cactus handler if it is a cactus. Don't be alarmed if the soil ball falls into pieces and you end up with a bare-root plant. This often happens and the plant will be fine once it is planted.

Put the plant in position. If the top of the soil ball is higher than your final planned surface, remove the plant and gently crumble soil away from the bottom until it will fit at the right level. Scoop some soil mix around the plant to hold it in position and tamp it in. Use a tamping tool around cacti to keep from getting pricked.

7. Following the same procedure, place your other plants. If the container is large, place the major banking elements as you work. Keep in mind that a rather stark, open feeling is your goal. Fill in with soil mix and tamp as you progress until all of the plants have been placed. Fill any low spots and tamp the entire surface well with the tamping tool or your fingers.

8. Add the final surface elements. You may want to give the entire surface or some areas a light sprinkling of sand. A dry riverbed can be added from small gravel or sand, with banks of rocks. Most surface elements should be slightly buried as if the wind had blown around them. Use a watercolor brush or pencil point to clean the plants.

9. Give the terrarium a very light watering with the bulb sprayer, just

The Wonderful World of Cacti and Succulents • 93

The completed desert scene, ready to enhance a sunny location

enough to settle and slightly moisten the soil. Cover the entire surface evenly. Clean the outside of the container if it needs it.

10. Since there is no moisture balance to set up, just put your topless terrarium in a sunny spot and enjoy it.

General Information, Maintenance, and Tips

Desert terrariums will need watering but not overwatering, which is the only sure way to damage these plants. Use a bulb sprayer and room-temperature water for all watering; a direct stream of poured water may badly damage a desert scene. During the growing and flowering season (March through September) apply water once a week, twice a week if there is a hot spell or the plants look dehydrated. From October to February, a light watering every other week is adequate for cacti. During this time continue to give the succulents a light weekly watering. When you water, the soil should receive a thorough moistening, but not a drenching. The succulents can be given a bit more water than the cacti, since with the bulb sprayer you can control the amount of water going to each plant. Above all, remember that it is far easier to damage these plants by overwatering than by underwatering.

A long hot summer spell calls for a bit of extra water. Accordingly, gray winter days mean less water is needed, so adjust your schedule to the conditions outdoors. Be sure the soil mix is thoroughly dry between waterings.

Some succulents, such as echeverias, tend to lose their leaves from the bottom. This might mean a bit more water is needed, but is usually a natural growth pattern. Don't become alarmed and douse the plant with water. If *all* leaves show signs of withering, water is needed.

Desert terrariums can profit from an overall light fertilizing with a water-soluble, organic fertilizer during the growing season. Use one-half the strength given on the package and apply with the bulb sprayer when a regular watering is due. Fertilize once in April or May and again six to eight weeks later. Use the same amount of fertilizer water as you would use plain water.

Getting cacti to flower indoors is a bit tricky. We are generally happy just with the plants. If you want to try, give them a *very* dry, cool winter period with temperatures from 50° to 60°. This is necessary for the buds to form, and decreased light can also be helpful. When new growth or

Even on a snowy day, desert terrariums enjoy full light

buds start to appear, increase the water supply to once a week, make sure they receive sunlight, and fertilize lightly as directed above. You may be treated to some brilliant cactus flowers.

A lack of color in leaves and shoots, or elongated growth are the usual signs that more light is needed.

Warm, sunny days and cool nights are ideal conditions for the desert terrarium. A sunny window provides the best approximation of these conditions, and your plants will be very happy there. Do not put desert plants over a radiator as the extra heat is detrimental during winter months.

Most desert plants are slow growers, so don't think they are unhealthy because they don't increase in size. They also rest during a considerable part of the year.

Creating Layers of Color

All you need to create fascinating layers of color for your desert terrarium are stiff paper, tape, a range of colored materials, and a simple method. This project follows the regular desert planting procedure, with the layering done as a part of step 4.

To make the layers, first cut a piece of stiff paper to the height of your container. Placing it inside of the container, adjust it so that it is about ½ inch smaller on all sides than the exterior walls of the terrarium. Then remove it and tape the ends together to make a rigid "dam." The dam will be round, rectangular, or cone-shaped, according to the shape of your container. The cone is used for containers with inward sloping sides, such as a brandy snifter, and the wide end of the cone should be cut to sit evenly on a flat surface.

After you have completed steps 1 through 3, place the dam on top of the soil separator. (See photo.) Prepare your soil mix and spoon about ¾ inch inside the dam. You are now ready to start layering in the space between the dam and the container walls. You can use a variety of materials for this effect, some of which you may color yourself. Soil does not come in bright purples, reds, blues, and greens and we don't think your terrarium should come in those colors either.

A terrarium can bring the beauty of
a woodland scene into your home

Hanging terrariums are
best viewed near eye level

This comment-producing
coffee-table terrarium
is both useful and
decorative

A bookcase is an excellent place to display a collection of terrariums

A bottle garden on its side will bring admiration and questions

A well-designed bottle garden, made with patience and special tools

Simplicity and elegance — one miniature African
violet in a decorative container

Terrariums make a beautiful centerpiece to brighten any meal

A "layered" desert planting, which should receive direct sunlight

Sun-loving lizards, cacti and succulents share this desert vivarium

Sun basking is a favorite activity of these desert dwellers

Creating a layered effect is easy with the use of a paper dam

The following colors can be made of natural undyed materials:

Dark brown — sterilized potting soil
Medium brown — prepackaged cactus soil
Gray — clay kitty litter (this also comes in a light orange shade)
Yellow — sharp sand
White — white sand, available at tropical fish stores
Tan — vermiculite

It is also possible to make colored sand by dyeing either sand or vermiculite with food coloring, which you can buy at the supermarket. White sand will produce lighter, clearer colors; sharp sand and vermiculite will be darker.

The formulas below will dye one cup for each color. Put the coloring into a can or glass and add water — 2 tablespoons for sand, 4 tablespoons for vermiculite. Add the material to be colored and stir well to distribute the color. Allow the material to dry out for an hour or two before using it; however some colors may lose intensity if not put into a terrarium within twenty-four hours. Here are the proportions:

Brown — 2 teaspoons red, ½ teaspoon yellow, ½ teaspoon blue
Orange — 1 teaspoon yellow, 1 teaspoon red
Mustard — 1 teaspoon red, 1 teaspoon yellow, ½ teaspoon blue
Yellow — 2 teaspoons yellow
Olive — ½ teaspoon each of red, blue, and yellow

a. White sand is placed for the lightest coloring
b. Soil and colored sand are used for other layers

Use a soup or serving spoon to start filling in the space between the dam and the container walls with small portions of different colors. (See above.) Build highs and lows and try for smooth separation lines. You can use the spoon handle to smooth the top of each layer before the next one goes in. As you place the colors, also add soil mix inside the dam to keep the two approximately even. Keep adding layers of different colors to suit your own design ideas until the material is about 1 inch from the top. Make sure the levels inside and outside of the dam are the same.

The finished terrarium, a great showpiece or gift

c. When the layering is completed, the dam is removed
d. Regular procedures are used to finish the planting

At this point you are ready to remove the dam. Grasp it firmly with both hands and pull it, slowly but steadily, straight up. It will come out easily, leaving your layers intact. Add desert soil mix almost to the final planned level and return to the regular procedure for steps 5 to 10. Easy, isn't it?

9 Bottle Gardens

The most knock-out, gee-whiz, how-did-you-do-it terrarium is one in a narrow-neck bottle. We can easily tell you how to create this awe-inspiring specimen, but we can't honestly tell you it's a snap. This is our "we hope you have a lot of patience and a steady hand" chapter.

A neighbor recently brought us a dying bottle garden constructed according to four paragraphs of instructions. It had no drainage, insufficient soil depth, and incompatible plants. The instructions read, "if the plants need water, add some" — which is no help at all. Planting a narrow-neck container cannot be described in a few paragraphs; this entire chapter is devoted to giving you *full*, step-by-step instructions for making a spectacular, successful garden in a bottle. Most of these steps are not new. What is new is the *procedure* for placing elements inside the bottle, since everything that goes into this terrarium requires the use of tools.

Choose your narrow-neck container carefully. For your first undertaking a neck diameter of 2 inches should be the minimum. A 3-inch opening makes planting easier, but anything larger destroys the illusion that you have spirited full-grown plants into the interior of a bottle. After you become experienced in working with tools, you can work down to bottles with smaller openings. Wine, cider, and liquor bottles are good for later projects, as are the classic five-gallon water bottle and other deco-

101

A thriving narrow-neck container,
placed under a cascading Boston fern

Three bottle-garden containers:
¾-inch opening (hard), 2¾-inch
(easiest), and 2-inch (medium)

OUCH

Cacti are not narrow-neck
terrarium plants

rative bottles with openings as small as ¾ inch. For your first attempt, look for a container in the half-gallon to two-gallon capacity. The container we used is a chemist's flask that holds about one and one-half gallons and has a 2¼-inch opening, excellent for a first planting.

If you decide to use a bottle-garden kit, be sure the neck opening is at least 2 inches wide. In our experience, the soil mixes of these kits can benefit from the addition of peat moss and especially perlite. Kit instructions are often sketchy and the ones we give here will greatly simplify your planting.

Use any plants from the tropical list that will fit into your container. Most plants are not damaged by having their leaves folded upward. To determine whether a plant will fit, make a circle with your thumb and forefinger around the base of the plant and bring it upward to see if all the foliage will pass through. Many woodland plants cannot pass this test without damage, especially ferns. If you want to do a woodland narrow-neck, look for a bottle with a 3-inch opening. Don't use any plants from the desert list; cacti and succulents are not for bottle gardens. When making plant selections, plan for a lush, full effect, but allow room for growth as pruning in a narrow-neck is tricky.

Narrow–Neck Planting Tools

Diamonds may be a girl's best friend, but for a bottle-garden planter proper tools are more valuable than jewels. In assembling earlier terrariums you used a few basic planting tools; now you are totally dependent upon them for all planting. This may seem obvious, but remember that all your tools must fit through the neck of your bottle.

Three tools are especially valuable in planting narrow-neck containers: a mechanical grabber, terrarium tongs, and number 12 grade TW electric wire. The mechanical grabber is fantastically helpful for placing plants, moving surface elements, and making all kinds of adjustments. Basically a mechanic's tool used to pick up small items in hard-to-reach places, it works equally well in reverse — to *put* objects in hard-to-reach places, such as inside your bottle. It can be purchased in garden centers, plant stores, variety stores, and auto mechanic supply stores. The grabber sometimes comes in terrarium tool kits, where it may be called a "pick-up tool" or "terrarium tool."

Next to the grabber, number 12 grade TW electrical wire is the most valuable and versatile tool we have found. It bends easily into any shape, but is rigid enough for digging and other tasks. Any wire with these qualities can be substituted, but this wire is readily available at hardware stores or electrical supply houses. Since it is cheap, buy a 4-foot or 6-foot piece and shape it into several different tools, or have different lengths for different-sized bottles.

Flexible electrical wire is an extremely versatile tool

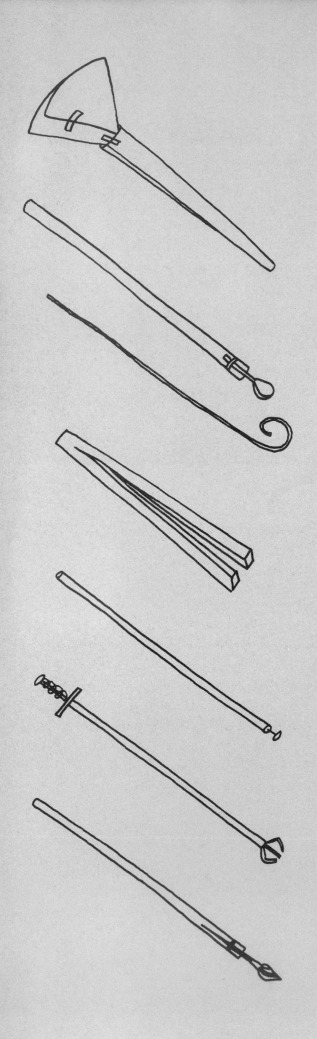

Terrarium tongs are really a pair of giant tweezers and do many of the same jobs as the mechanical grabber. They are available in stores that carry terrarium supplies and sometimes come in terrarium kits.

Here is a full list of useful tools for narrow-neck terrarium work:

Funnel. A two-part assembly made from heavy paper and tape works best. It will keep the container walls clean during planting. When resting in the container neck, the bottom of the funnel should be 1 inch higher than the planned final surface; if it is too long, cut off a portion.

Digger. This is made by taping a small plastic spoon to the end of a dowel. Cut the sides of the spoon if it won't fit. Number 12 grade TW electrical wire with a bent end will also work as a digger.

Mover. Terrarium tongs, or your digger if you don't have these.

Tamper. You can use a thumbtack or small cork on the end of a dowel, the blunt end of a knitting needle, or the wrong end of the terrarium tongs.

Placer. The mechanical grabber works best; terrarium tongs can also be used.

Cleaner. A long-handled artist's brush, a watercolor brush taped to a dowel, or paper toweling on the end of the electrical wire will all work.

Scissors. These are used for cutting the soil separator and trimming plants before planting if necessary.

Watering device. A variable-head plant mister is best, but a bulb sprayer or empty spray-type glass cleaner bottle can be used.

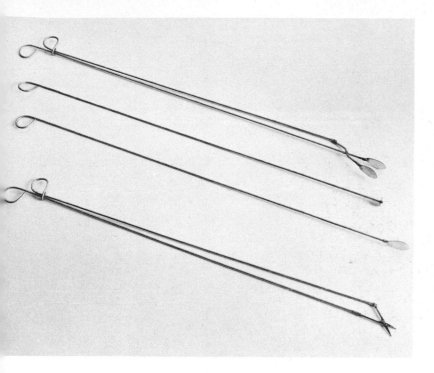

With these tools from A&N Terrarium Tool
Company, planting a five-gallon container
is greatly simplified

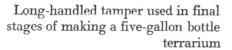

Long-handled tamper used in final
stages of making a five-gallon bottle
terrarium

One last word about tools: be independent. If you find a way to do a job easier than the way we suggest, use it. Whatever works best for you is the best way.

The shopping list for your narrow-neck project is the same as that for the first terrarium, with the addition of the tools discussed above. Remember that natural decorative elements as well as plants must fit through your bottle opening. The amount of drainage material, charcoal, and soil mix must be increased to meet the size of your container. Three times the amount used on your first project would be right for a two-gallon container.

Plant It Up!

Before you start, read through the entire planting procedure. Plan to spend one to two hours on this project. We find it's a good idea to take a break after the first few plants are in to steady our nerves before the final steps and to see how our arrangement is progressing.

1. Give your container a good cleaning. Stubborn spots on the inside can be scrubbed off with a bit of steel wool or kitchen scouring pad secured to the flexible wire. Rinse to remove all soap or detergent. Empty out the excess water and let the bottle stand upside down for ten minutes. Then stand it upright to dry out. Do this a few hours before planting, or dust and soil particles will adhere to the damp walls. When the container is dry, assemble all of your material on a well-lighted work space, with papers underneath.

2. Using your two-part funnel, add drainage material and then charcoal. For the 1½-gallon container we used about 1 inch of drainage and 3 table-spoons of charcoal. A five-gallon bottle will take 1½ inches of drainage and ½ cup of charcoal.

3. Cut your soil separator to lie flat on the drainage layer and barely reach the edges of the container. This may take a try or two, so stay on the large side for the first cut. To place the soil separator, roll it up and push it through the neck. Use the flexible wire to unroll and place it. If it's too large, remove

106

it with the mechanical grabber, recut, and replace.

4. Prepare the tropical soil mix according to the instructions in chapter 4. Allow six cups for a one-gallon container. It's better to make too much than not enough, because you add soil as you plant and don't want to run out. Crumble any lumps so they do not clog the funnel.

Put the funnel in position and spoon in the soil mix to about two-thirds the planned depth. You may have to use the flexible wire to break up a clog or two. In our sample the first layer was 1 inch deep. You will add more mix as you plant, but putting it all in now makes the planting more difficult. This may be different from other instructions you have seen, but it considerably simplifies planting. Use the flexible wire to spread the soil; don't shake the bottle.

5. Roughly plan the design on your work surface, with the plants still in their pots. Practically all narrow-neck terrariums are round and should be designed to be seen from all sides, but your design can't be too exact, because you can't always get plants precisely where you want them. Don't worry about this, just figure out a general arrangement. The final designing will be done while you are doing the planting. Fill-in by growth is usually quick.

6. Make a hole for the largest plant with your digger, right down to the soil separator. Remove the plant from its pot and gently crumble away as much

107

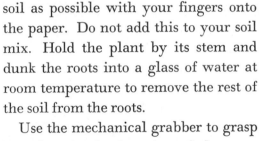

soil as possible with your fingers onto the paper. Do not add this to your soil mix. Hold the plant by its stem and dunk the roots into a glass of water at room temperature to remove the rest of the soil from the roots.

Use the mechanical grabber to grasp the plant at the junction of the roots and stem. Work the roots into the neck of the bottle with your fingers, then lower the plant into the hole you have prepared. At this point it is very helpful to have a spouse, lover, or close friend around or to be ambidextrous. That's because it's much easier to anchor the plant if you use two tools. Hold the plant in place with the grabber while you shovel soil mix around the roots with your digger. If you are doing it alone, you may have to shift from one tool to the other. This is the real test of patience, for sometimes the plant seems to take on a life of its own. Remember that you are smarter than the plant and will win out in the end.

Firm the soil mix around the plant with the tamper to hold it in place. You may give this plant a few knocks while you are placing the others, so try to get it well anchored.

7. Follow the same procedure for the other plants. Dig a hole, remove the soil, lower the plant into position, anchor it, and tamp the soil. If you find you need more soil after placing the second or third plant, add some through the funnel. As you pour try to position the soil mix around the plants already in place. Follow these steps until all of the plants are in position. Then give the entire surface a thorough tamping, add more soil mix through the funnel where needed, and re-tamp well.

8. Now you are ready to place your decorative surface elements and smaller ground cover. You can use moss if it is cut into pieces small enough to fit in the bottle neck. Tamp it into the soil mix well. Easy-rooting ground covers such as selaginella or creeping pilea can be divided into small portions and pushed into the soil mix where they will soon begin growing.

Use different-toned rocks, pebbles, seed pods, and other natural materials to complete the terrarium. They can be dropped in or lowered by the mechanical grabber. Place them somewhat haphazardly around the outer areas. Avoid anything that might mildew, unless you have baked it. By now you know that plastic elves devour plants so you won't use any. Give the terrarium a final appraisal and make minor

The finished bottle garden takes its place for a long, comment-provoking life

changes if needed. Straighten any leaning plants and re-tamp. Add lighter colors of gravel or sand if the surface needs emphasis.

9. The first part of the cleaning step is to remove as much dust as possible from the container sides and plants with a long brush and a paper towel secured to the flexible wire. Really work at this, because the amount of water needed to clean the sides and plants will produce far too much moisture in the container. Your cleaning must be done before you water. Clean the outside at this time to make inside spots easier to see.

A final washing down of the walls and plants then follows with water from a sprayer. A plant mister with a variable head is best because it allows you to aim a single stream of water to any problem spots. Direct the spray to all sides of the terrarium, especially the lower portions, and try to wash down the sides as you spray. Don't use any more water than you need to provide the moisture for your terrarium because airing out a narrow-neck container can take a long time. The soil should be evenly moistened by this spraying, but not soaked. For our sample we used one cup. Because of the small opening, some bottle gardens remain healthy without a cork. This does not establish a true water cycle and means you will eventually have to add water, so we always use the cork or other top with an occasional fifteen-minute airing.

110

10. Place the terrarium in its new location. For the next week or so you must check it daily to see how the moisture cycle is doing. A light daily misting is desired. Constant heavy misting means the bottle should be left open for several days. Very heavy misting means excess water is present and should be wiped off the container sides with a paper towel on the end of a flexible wire. Do this immediately to prevent rot. If there is no mist at all, add a teaspoon of water every third day until the desired misting level is achieved.

Soon you will see a happy, healthy look to your new terrarium, and after two or three weeks you may see new growth appearing. Then it's time to give yourself a pat on the back for your skill and patience and move on to another narrow-neck idea. It may be a very small one, with only one or two plants and some ground cover, or a giant five-gallon water jug.

If you want a *real* challenge, try a narrow-neck on its side. This *more* than doubles the difficulty, and a 3-inch opening will be very welcome. To build it, prop the container at a slight angle, with the neck 3 or 4 inches higher than the bottom. Follow the instructions in this chapter, but use horizontal rather than vertical movements. For instance, after the drainage, charcoal, and soil separator are in, the soil mix must be spooned and pushed into the bottle. When you have completed this project, you will know that you have succeeded in the most difficult of all terrarium forms.

A well-designed terrarium brings a section of nature right into your home, as does the woodland scene in this fifteen-gallon aquarium from Metaframe

10 Design Ideas for Large Terrariums

This is a coffee or cocktail chapter, which means pleasant reading, but no actual planting. Before you begin to assemble a large terrarium, you should have a definite, well-planned landscape design.

Small and medium-sized terrariums have limited design possibilities. You can use only three to six plants, a ground cover, and a few natural surface elements. How well you use these certainly does make a difference in the appearance of the finished terrarium. Still, if you take three healthy specimens and plant them properly in an attractive container, the terrarium is going to look good — because the container itself is often the most predominant design element.

In a large container a fundamental change occurs in the relationship between the container and its contents. The design of the planting becomes increasingly more important and the appearance of the container becomes less important. Structurally, the large container is usually simple, not decorative: a plain rectangle, sphere, or cylinder. Also, the larger size allows the planting to take on its own identity. The terrarium is no longer dependent upon the container for its looks, but assumes a personality of its own — plant liberation!

Let's give an illustration. On the following page are two terrariums. The small pitcher is very charming. We made it and think it's extremely attractive, but there is no denying that the container itself is

Ambassador

the most eye-catching part of the total effect. In contrast, the fish-tank terrarium draws your interest to the interior — the plants, rocks, composition, and naturalness of the scene. In a large terrarium the predominant interest should be in the planting.

Of course a large terrarium requires more of everything: more drainage, more soil mix, more plants, and, most of all, more cerebral activity beforehand. Although you have to do more advance planning and take extra care in choosing plants, natural elements, and the container, there's a great plus in large terrariums; they allow room for experimenting, making changes, and trying out new ideas. When they are completed their appearance well warrants the extra effort.

114 • *Planting Procedures and Maintenance*

The pitcher terrarium, one of many
well-designed containers from Pilgrim
Glass, is extremely attractive;
the larger terrarium is simpler, but
allows a greater freedom of design

Planning Your Landscape

The first step is a combined decision as to environment, container, and
location. The natural, airy quality of a woodland terrarium shows up best
in an aquarium tank. The varied foliage and lush collage effect of the
tropical environment is well suited to spheres and giant brandy snifters.
For a sunny location, a desert scene in any of these containers offers an
unusual and dramatic approach to plant grouping. In addition, such
finds as large pickle or other food jars, specially constructed glass or
plastic rectangles, or anything else you discover that is waterproof, trans-

Samples of containers you can use for large terrariums

parent, and suited to its location can be used. Any of these that you do not have around the house will be readily available at garden centers, plant stores, and department stores.

Many large containers come without covers, so you must provide these unless you are building a desert scene. Decorative tops can sometimes be purchased separately for round containers; if not, one can be cut to order from ⅛-inch glass. Aquarium covers should be cut from ³⁄₁₆-inch glass to fit inside the top frame. An alternative is to remove the frame and rest the glass cover on the top of the four sides, which creates a simple, clean look. To remove the frame, carefully pry the support from the glass with a paring knife or other small knife. Work the frame *upward* from the four corners, until it can be lifted off. Be sure to keep all pressure upward to avoid any leverage against the glass. If the aquarium has corner braces or seems to be *very* firmly glued down, it is best to leave it on rather than risk breaking a side. Excess adhesive can be cleaned with a single-edged razor blade and steel wool. Be careful when moving the glass top, if the frame has been removed, so as not to tip it into the terrarium.

The selection of a large terrarium container depends to a considerable degree on where you intend to place it. A planted fifteen-gallon aquarium may easily weigh sixty pounds, and a 16-inch sphere may weigh thirty pounds. In addition to providing proper light conditions, your location must be able to support the weight of the completed terrarium. Choose a permanent location for these terrariums, because they are not something you can pick up and move around when you do the dusting.

General Design and Layout

When the initial environment-container-location decision has been made, the next step is a blueprint or vivid mental image of how you want the finished terrarium to look. If you are the type of person who likes to work from a floor plan or sketch, work out your ideas on paper. Make a rough perspective drawing or container outline. Decide where you want the larger plants, banking elements, rivers, and rocks. Then fill in the medium-sized and smaller plants. Take this along when you go shopping so you can pick plants for specific locations.

Another approach is to start out with a rough plan in mind and the approximate number and sizes of the plants you will need. Then you can buy the best-looking ones available for your environment. Be sure to assemble them together in the store before you make your purchase to see if you can improve on your selections. It's a lot easier to make a switch at this stage than after you have brought them all home. Buy an extra small plant or two to have on hand. If they are not needed you can use them in another planting.

Whichever of these procedures you use, your first design consideration is where to position the largest plant and the largest surface element. An excellent position for the dominant plant is a raised or banked area. This will usually place it toward the back of the container. Banking can be done with rocks, cork, bark, or sections of tree branches. If you want a very high bank, you may have to use a good solid rock or two at the base

In building a bank, the retaining wall must be held in position while soil is tamped to support it

In laying out your design either a perspective sketch or a floor plan can be used. Below is the terrarium built from these two designs

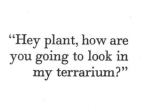

"Hey plant, how are you going to look in my terrarium?"

of the "cliff" to support the banking material. These rocks can be partially exposed or completely buried, depending on your final design. All banking should be done at a slight angle since vertical banks are rarely found in nature; they also may topple over. An inclined slope is much more effective, and low, subdued banking looks best in a desert terrarium.

Four qualities will determine the way you use plants as design elements. When you look at a plant you should say, "Hey plant, what are you going to look like in my terrarium? What have you got to offer me as to volume, figure, looks, and complexion?" That means size, shape, texture, and color.

Size is the most important consideration, and certainly the easiest to understand. Your terrarium should have a selection of small, medium, and large plants. "Large" in a terrarium is a relative term; it may mean a 3-inch plant in one terrarium and a 10-inch plant in another. Fortunately, the plants we have listed come in a range of sizes, and although they certainly will grow, none should grow so rapidly as to cause a problem. One great asset of a large terrarium is the greater latitude of plant selection you get from the increased space. There is no exact ratio that can be followed for mixing plant sizes, but a general rule is always to have one plant that is dominant. In very large terrariums two plants can be used as focal points, but one should still be predominant. A terrarium with plants all the same size is dull, dull, dull.

Shape is the next consideration. Alas, there will be no Mae West or Mark Spitz plants in your terrarium, but we still must consider their shape. Plants come in irregular, symmetrical, globular, tall, spreading, bushy, and lots of other shapes. That's perfect, because varied shapes as well as sizes make an interesting terrarium. Cylindrical, treelike, and upright plants are usually placed in the background, low-growing ones in the foreground, and round, bushy, and other similar shapes in the middle areas.

Examples of plants showing a range of textures: *from left, Asparagus plumosus,* maidenhair fern, peperomia "Emerald Ripple," sansevieria "Hahnii," and ball cactus

Texture covers such plant characteristics as leaf size and structure, branching habits, rough or smooth leaves, light or heavy effect. This is the most difficult plant quality to explain and is best shown in the photograph above.

Achieving a balance of textures is one of the most important and perhaps most challenging aspects of design. Every plant in your terrarium should have a different look; the goal is variety with a feeling of harmony and contrast. What constitutes a proper contrast? This is a matter for your eye, your personal sense of design, and the total planned scene. As you work with plants you will see that some look better together than others. That is learning to design with texture.

Color is a design factor which should not cause any problems. There are a few plants with high color such as iresene and the peacock plant, and many with variegated leaves in shades of green, white, yellow, and pink. They are all marvelous in a terrarium as long as you remember that the more color a plant has, the more light it usually needs. Basically a terrarium is a range of greens, and if you have balanced size, shape, and texture, it is almost certain that you will have a good range of plant colors. You don't have to worry about color co-ordination, because nature has designed the plants so that leaf colors do not clash, particularly among plants from the same environment. The only color designing you should do is to make sure that plants with highly colored or variegated leaves are equally distributed and not bunched up. Even the desert plants that range into earth tones such as grays, browns, and reds blend together easily.

The wonderful and subtle hues of plants in combination with the surface color and natural elements provide all the color needed in a terrarium. One of the reasons we are so opposed to artificial colors and "cute" additions to terrariums is that they detract from the natural beauty found in a well-designed terrarium. These extras are often thrown in to cover up the fact that the terrarium has been tossed together with no thought of design or plant harmony. If you create a well-designed terrarium from natural elements, you will never need the use of these distracting additions.

Choosing Natural Decorative Elements

Large terrariums need more and larger natural elements. Collecting them should be in the back of your mind as you walk around your neighborhood, on vacations, and during outings. You may even want to make a special collection trip if you are a city dweller. All natural elements are gifts from nature, and we have two absolute rules about collecting them. One: Never take any *living* material from a park or public grounds. This is stealing from the others who come to enjoy these areas. Two: When collecting moss, lichen, or other small plants on privately owned land, take only what you can use immediately. If you see a fair amount of a living specimen around, it is permissible to take a small sample. If you have any doubt, give the plant a chance and leave it alone.

Many materials that appear on the surface of a forest, pastureland, or even desert area can be used in a terrarium. Small rocks, stones, gravel, and pebbles are excellent. Look for flat rocks that can be used to build banks. Acorns, seed pods, thistles, and other means of plant reproduction are our favorites. Look for sections of fallen branches that can be used as banking material. They often will have moss or even small plants growing on them. This brings up a very important problem that can occur with natural elements — fungus and mildew. To be perfectly honest, we don't always bake every organic element that we place in terrariums. But we are terrarium nuts; we check them every day and are willing to remove anything that starts showing signs of these problems,

Some possible banking
materials

or we go through the efforts of spraying with a fungicide. We think you
will be much better off doing as we tell you to do, not as we do. This
means baking all organic matter going into a closed terrarium for two
hours in a 250° oven. The problem comes when you find a branch
covered with moss, which would be killed by baking. As a devoted
terrarium builder, are you willing to take the chance of problems for the
opportunity to use such a great find? That decision we leave to you.

Leaves are another mixed blessing. We really like a few scattered
around, but they can also become moldy and baking usually dries them
out to the point of disintegration. We have had excellent luck with leaves
from both broad-leaved and needled evergreen trees and shrubs. They
stand up very well in terrariums and do not seem to rot or mildew, as
many deciduous leaves are apt to do.

One man-made object we do like in our terrariums is a marvelous
ceramic mushroom. Each one is handmade, very realistic, and has a dull
finish instead of the usual shiny one. Such reproductions are hard to find,
but can be used to add to the natural look if they also are natural looking.
We have not been able to locate satisfactory life-sized, realistic frogs,
toads, lizards, or any animal forms. If you find some, let us know.

Do's, Don'ts, and Other Tips

Here is a run-through of helpful ideas:

For a large terrarium we like to produce a quantity of darkened perlite.
Since the food- or meat-coloring method is a bit difficult and expensive
for a large amount, we make a whole bucketful with ordinary black or

dark brown fabric dye. Follow the package instructions, but use just enough water to moisten the perlite well. Do this in a metal bucket or one you don't mind discoloring. Stir the perlite around with a stick and let it sit overnight. Strain it when you take it out of the bucket and lightly wash off the excess dye with a hose or in the sink. The perlite will come out a light gray or brown that will blend into the color of your soil mix. This may sound like a lot of trouble, but it's really very quick and simple. If you're making a number of terrariums, or even a few large ones, the bucketful will be used rapidly. Unlike other tinted perlite, it loses very little color when it dries.

Desert terrariums have different design requirements from their woodland and tropical cousins, as they reflect the bare look of a semi-arid or arid region. A desert planting should be sparser, with subdued terracing and more emphasis on bare ground. Use a surface covering of sand if you want to create a drier look. Wind-dried wood, thistles, one or two dried leaves, rocks, and pebbles will all add to this scene, but exercise restraint. Use of plants should also be somewhat sparse, but be sure to take advantage of the wide variety of sizes and shapes offered by cacti and succulents. Grouping should be random, never evenly spaced. A focal point in a desert terrarium might be a dramatic rock rather than a plant. Don't forget the technique of layering colors for extra drama.

We are often asked if it is possible to mix plants from the different environments. In the case of desert plants, the answer is NO! These plants are very hardy and easy to care for, but must be given the conditions of a desert and are as totally unsuited to a tropical or woodland scene as plants from those two environments are to a desert setting. The question of mixing tropical and woodland plants is more difficult to answer. Since the tropical list contains some of the hardiest plants

Woodland natural surface elements

Desert natural surface elements

around and the conditions of the tropical and woodland terrariums have similarities, the plants are probably going to do all right. We happen to prefer the more consistent look of plants that live together naturally. If you want to mix, you are better off putting a tropical plant in a woodland terrarium than vice versa, since the woodland plants are a little more particular about their conditions. The final decision should be made after considering the plants' needs and the effect you want. As an example, a sansevieria "Hahnii" would survive but would look rather silly mixed in with ferns and moss; but a small fittonia could be very nice. Partridge-berry would not only look out of place in a tropical setting but might suffer from the soil mix and warmer temperatures.

Large terrariums can often be highlighted by one, or possibly more, flowering plants. These will need the brightest light you can provide short of direct sunlight, and will do best under artificial light. They have some special requirements, may increase your care a bit, but are generally very rewarding when in bloom. Their specific needs are discussed in the chapter on flowering plants.

Another way you can use your large terrarium is to experiment with plants other than the ones listed. Many will succeed; some won't. Ask at your favorite plant source for some suggestions. After you plant the new specimens, keep an eye on them for their response and remove them if they obviously do not like a terrarium as a home. You will soon develop a sixth sense about terrariums that will allow you to choose those that will succeed.

11 Planting a Large Terrarium

For a real afficionado, planting a large terrarium is like pitching a World Series game after the regular season. You get to use more and larger plants, many elements from nature, embankments, "streams," and the other expanded design ideas discussed in the previous chapter. More than ever it becomes possible to create an enchanting scene from nature in your home.

Because of their similarities in assembly, the instructions that follow are for woodland and tropical scenes. If your choice is a desert terrarium, follow these instructions, but make adjustments in soil mix, light, plant selection, watering, and the finishing touches.

Our photographed example is a tropical scene in an 18-inch-high brandy snifter. We think an aquarium is better for a woodland setting; a desert planting works in either one. The number of plants on the shopping list is an estimate, intended as a starting point if this is the first time you have planted a large container. It's always a good idea to buy a few extra small plants to use as fillers. The tropical planting needs enough plants to achieve a lush, massed effect. The woodland scene, with more open ground, needs more ground-cover plants, mosses, and natural elements. Desert landscapes should be sparse; the number of plants can vary greatly because of their incredible variety in size, shape, and structure.

The completed large terrarium in an 18-inch-high brandy snifter from Riekes Crisa

Shopping List and Preparations

As an experienced terrarium builder, you probably have many of the items for this project on hand. Run through the list and check off what you need to pick up, so you don't get stuck without peat moss just as you start into a Sunday afternoon assembly.

Container	*10-gallon aquarium*	*16- to 18-inch sphere*
Drainage	4 to 5 quarts	2 to 3 quarts
Charcoal	¾ cup	½ cup
Soil mix	10 to 12 quarts woodland mix	6 to 8 quarts tropical mix
Plants	2 large (6 to 8 inches)	2 large (5 to 7 inches)
	3 medium (3 to 6 inches)	4 medium (2 to 5 inches)
	4 small or ground-cover plants	2 small or ground-cover plants

Soil separator — fiber glass or other synthetic material

Cleaning materials — glass cleaner, paper towels
Watering device — plant mister, bulb sprayer or empty spray-type
    glass cleaner bottle
Tools — large spoon, tamper, scissors, watercolor brush, razor blade
    (used for aquariums)
Natural elements — moss, rocks, seed pods, small branches
Banking materials — flat rocks, bark, branches
Bucket or large mixing bowl

Planting a large terrarium will take several hours. Plan it for a weekend afternoon or a full evening when you can work without interruptions and really enjoy the experience. Turn on some quiet plant music and invite someone to join you for companionship, advice, and assistance. Take your time and don't be in a hurry to finish. This terrarium is going to be around for a long time, and an extra half hour spent in creating a better planting will mean that much more enjoyment from the final result.

You need plenty of work space for this project. A large table in your back yard, workroom, or garage is ideal because you can spread out and don't have to worry about spills and clean-up. Lacking this, use a breakfast table or kitchen counter covered with newspapers.

Large desert terrariums can be made in a variety of containers, such as this impressive 16-inch globe

Step-by-Step Procedure

1. Give your container a thorough cleaning. Large containers are hard to clean in a sink, and there is greater chance for breakage. We advise a spray-type glass cleaner. In the case of aquariums, it may be necessary to use a single-edge razor blade to scrape excess adhesive off the glass. This is especially true if you remove the top frame. When your container is clean, assemble it and all other elements on the work surface. Double-check your list so you can concentrate on planting instead of hunting for tools.

2. Place the drainage material in the bottom of the container. Sprinkle the required amount of charcoal over it.

3. Cut your soil separator to fit over the drainage layer, reaching just to the edge of the glass.

4. Prepare the needed amount of soil mix in a large mixing bowl or bucket. It's always better to make plenty rather than end up short. Put in a layer 1½ to 2½ inches deep.

5. Arrange your plants and major design elements on the work surface. This dress rehearsal will give you a chance to check your total design idea, which may have been a floor plan, sketch, or visual image. If you find that some part doesn't look the way you planned, it's easy to make a major revision at this point but much harder

128

when you are halfway into the planting. Large banked areas and "streams" must be planned at this stage.

6. Begin your actual planting with the placement of the largest plant or banking element. Work from the back forward if your container is meant to be seen from one side. Start at the center and work outward for an "in the round" container, turning it as you work to make sure all sides are developing as planned. If you have a large plant behind a good-sized embankment, work with the two together. Remove the plant from its pot, put it into position, add the banking, and then fill in with soil mix. Hold the wall in position while you tamp, and then anchor the wall or support it with a rock if necessary.

The placement of the first few elements is critical, because these are the dominant design factors and determine the positioning of the rest of your plants. Be sure to place them with care.

7. Position the other plants, working in descending order of size. Add additional soil and tamp as you go.

After about half the planting is done, take a break, relax, and study the progress to that point. Decide how you want the final steps to go. See if any adjustments need to be made to the elements already in place. Then go on with the remainder of the plants. Put each plant in position and study its effect on the total look before tamping, because now you are adding the details. Use the last few plants to take care of

129

any bare spots that you didn't count on. A river goes in toward the end of your planting, although the space for it must be planned from the beginning. When all of the plants and major surface elements are in place, give the entire surface a good tamping, add soil mix where needed, and re-tamp.

8. Add the natural decorative elements. You have probably used a rock, bark, or pieces of branches in the banking and planting procedure. Smaller-sized elements are used to round out the natural look. Ground covers such as moss, baby's tears, selaginella, and creeping pilea can be placed in the foreground areas. Seed pods, evergreen leaves and needles, pine cones, sand, and gravel are used as final touches. Check often as you complete this step to see where an adjustment or addition is needed. Don't forget to bury some elements or dribble a little soil mix around them. Stand back and give the whole scene an appreciative look.

9. Next is a general clean-up and watering. Use a watercolor brush to clean plant leaves, rocks, and other elements. With a dry paper towel, wipe the sides free of dust particles. Wrap the towel around the brush to get behind the plants, if necessary. Then give the sides and plants a gentle washing with your plant mister. You know that this step also provides the moisture necessary to set up the water cycle, so the amount used should be just enough to moisten the entire surface and turn the soil mix a medium-dark color (un-

130

less it's a desert terrarium, of course). For a ten-gallon aquarium you will need about 2½ cups of water; for a 16- to 18-inch globe about 1½ cups. Never pour a stream of water into a terrarium as it can cause instant erosion and wreck your arrangement. Misting takes only a few seconds longer, but cleans the entire terrarium and distributes the moisture evenly. It may take as long as 15 minutes for the moisture to penetrate down through the soil mix, so wait that long before adding more. Remember that underwatering is much better than overwatering and can be easily corrected in the first week of your terrarium's life. Wipe moisture off the container walls to avoid spots.

10. Place the completed terrarium in its new location. An aquarium usually needs two people to handle it. Don't try moving a ten-gallon size by yourself unless you have been doing a lot of weightlifting. Add the cover, sit down, and admire your new creation.

Over the next few days make adjustments to the moisture cycle, using the established guidelines. Moisture balance may take longer to establish in a large terrarium. Its greater collection of plants, surface area, and glass exposure makes the entire cycle more active. Slight fluctuations due to temperature, light, or other external conditions should not cause concern as long as the overall balance is maintained. While enjoying your terrarium, observe the misting level and make any necessary adjustments.

131

The finished terrarium, ready to be placed in position

12 Keeping Your Terrarium Healthy

A healthy terrarium is a happy terrarium. Once you have established the moisture balance in your miniature environment, the plants will be living in ideal surroundings, and only simple, occasional maintenance should be needed. We will cover these procedures in this chapter.

There is, however, one catch in this perfect arrangement. If they *do* get started, diseases, insects, and other plant problems also thrive in these ideal surroundings. The high humidity and lack of natural controls will accelerate their spread and growth. Therefore we have included a brief description of possible plant ills and what to do about them.

Your goal should be to maintain the status quo. Terrariums are meant to be viewed, and as you look at yours you should notice any changes that occur. Anything other than slight plant growth should immediately be analyzed and corrected.

Routine Maintenance Procedures

Moisture balance. The moisture cycle, once established, is almost totally self-perpetuating. External variables such as length of day, temperature, light intensity, or a change in location can cause short-term fluctuations.

A healthy, problem-free terrarium is
a constant source of pleasure to its owner

"You don't look well today"

These are generally no cause for alarm and will even out in the long run if your balance is correct. A lack of misting or a period of heavy condensation that lasts over a week should be corrected by the normal process of adding water or removing the top. A weekly fifteen-minute airing is a good idea if it is convenient.

Over a period of time some terrariums lose enough moisture to need additional water. This does not mean the moisture cycle has gone wrong, simply that a tiny amount has escaped each day and needs to be replaced. This can happen in a month or two, or maybe never. We have one terrarium in a very tight fruit jar that balanced perfectly the day after planting and has gone well over a year with exactly the same moisture level.

Plant growth control. You may start to see new growth in a terrarium about a month after planting it. Most of this will be slow. It will give your terrarium a fuller look. Occasionally there will be some crowding or a need to improve one plant's appearance. A method called "pinching back" is used to control shape and legginess. Pinching with your fingers is difficult in a terrarium, so we recommend the use of small scissors to cut back wayward branches — make them slightly shorter than you want them to be. Pinching makes for fuller and more compact plants. More drastic cutting back, or pruning, is called for only when a plant has really gotten out of bounds. Use it if leaves are pressing heavily against the container walls or into the neck of a bottle garden. In these instances, prune the entire plant back to a manageable size. Make the cuts at branch joints or just above a leaf. Remember that this plant is *very* healthy and is going to be up to these same tricks soon, so try to get it as small as possible without ruining its lines.

Overgrown or out-of-proportion
plants can be reshaped by a
simple pruning operation

Pruning or cutting back in narrow-neck bottles is done with an injector or single-edge razor blade taped to the end of a dowel. It may be necessary to use a second dowel or flexible wire as support for something to "saw" against. Be sure to remove any cuttings with the mechanical grabber, terrarium tongs, or a pin taped to the end of a dowel.

After a year or so, terrariums sometimes begin to look overgrown and crowded. This usually means not enough room was allowed at the initial planting, but it is hard to estimate how much growth will occur in a year. The best solution is to remove one or two plants to another terrarium and replace them with smaller ones. This requires special procedures, especially in a bottle garden. See the section on plant replacement in this chapter for complete instructions on removal and replanting.

Temperature. Normal living temperatures are fine for terrariums. Modern heating and air conditioning usually produce a daytime range of 65° to 80° and nighttime temperatures about 10° cooler. The interior of a sealed terrarium is protected against sudden temperature changes, drafts, and dryness. A drop to 50° or an increase to 85° is not dangerous as long as it does not last more than a day or two. In general, woodland environments like cooler temperatures, cacti like it hot with cooler winters, and tropical plants are tolerant of almost anything except very cold spells.

Light. The guide to light conditions in chapter 2 (page 18) should make it possible for you to put your terrarium in a location where it will receive proper light. You will recall that this is bright or medium light with no sun for closed environments, and direct sun or bright light for desert scenes. A bright-light location near a south window may turn into a sunny one during the winter months because of the lower position of the sun. In November, December, and January, one or two hours of sunlight a day will not hurt your terrarium because of the lowered light intensity. No repositioning is necessary for those months, but at other times of the year direct sunlight on closed terrariums should be avoided.

Fertilizing. After your terrarium has been prospering for a year, it may need fertilizing. This is called for if the plants have stopped showing new growth, could be fuller and a bit larger, or seem to need a bit of a pick-up. *Most* terrariums will not need fertilizing, certainly not in the first year, so be very sure that growth stimulation really is needed or you will have an overgrown jungle. After one year you can safely fertilize if the plants are not crowded or pressing against the container walls.

Fertilizer is most beneficial if applied during the spring months. Other times of the year are fine, but skip applications during the winter. Use only water-soluble, organic fertilizers, such as fish emulsion or a seaweed-based product. Mix according to the package instructions, but use *one quarter* of the recommended amount. Apply with a bulb sprayer or plant mister, but use just enough to barely moisten the plant's leaves and the surrounding soil. Not enough is much better than too much, and a second application can be given if no new growth appears in one month. Naturally you will have to re-establish the moisture cycle.

Cacti and succulents should be fertilized during the spring and summer growing season, that means once in April or May and once six to

After more than a year, this peperomia was pressing against the sides of its container. It is removed for use in a larger terrarium and replaced by a smaller plant. The renovated planting will go back into its location with an uncrowded, fresh look

136

eight weeks later. Any water-soluble, organic house-plant food can be used, diluted to *half* the strength recommended on the package. Mix with water and apply with a bulb mister when a regular watering is needed. A 10-5-5 fertilizer is excellent. This means that the fertilizer contains 10 percent nitrogen, 5 percent phosphorus, and 5 percent potassium.

Blooming plants need a special fertilizing program, which is described in the chapter on those plants.

Plant replacement. If a terrarium plant should die, become badly diseased or infected, or grow so large that you feel it should be moved to a larger container, you are going to have to remove it from the terrarium. In containers with openings large enough to admit your hand, use a spoon to reach under the plant and lift it out, including as much of the root ball as possible. Throw any unhealthy plant away. A healthy plant can be potted up for later use in another terrarium or placed in one right away. Remember it has been living under ideal conditions, so it will very likely show signs of shock if it is not put in a terrarium as soon as possible.

To remove a plant from a narrow-neck container, use a small plastic spoon taped to a dowel to loosen the plant, then grasp it with the mechanical grabber or terrarium tongs. Gently shake off as much soil as possible inside the container to avoid dirtying the sides of the bottle and the other leaves as you bring the plant through the neck, roots first. Use an artist's brush or paper towel on a flexible wire to clean the sides and

plants, if necessary. If you have to mist the inside to clean it, your garden will surely be overwatered and need considerable airing out to re-establish the water cycle.

You must then decide if you want to replace the plant. If you can reach inside the container, this is very easy. Naturally, don't do it if the terrarium is crowded and looks better as it is. In narrow-necked terrariums, we advise you not to try, because you would probably dirty the container walls and encounter considerable difficulty planting in an established garden. The potential damages are certain to be greater than the need for another plant. It is much better to smooth the surface and put in a few stones or a small stem cutting of an easily rooted ground cover. Use the same procedure for this as for the original planting. Moss is always a good alternative.

Insects, Diseases, and Other Problems

As we mentioned before, few terrariums develop any of the problems listed below, but once started they will really take off. Most plants that you bring home will be insect free. If you are the super-cautious type, give them a few light bursts of a general-purpose indoor insect spray (recommended brands are Plantabbs, Swiss Farms, and Ortho) and wait two days before planting. No matter what you do, there may be dormant insects or eggs in the soil or on the foliage that cannot be detected until they start causing trouble. Proper care in selecting healthy plants, choosing soil mix ingredients, and the lack of access into a closed container will prevent most problems. If you are going to have trouble it will probably occur within a month after planting. After that you can be almost positive everything will remain healthy.

In the following discussion we have listed the most usual and first seen symptom, then the cause of the trouble, and finally its cure. If you see something that is not right in your terrarium, skim down the list of symptoms until you find the one that describes your situation, learn the trouble, and apply the remedy.

All or several plants drooping, turning yellow, or losing leaves. Although you should check for wide-spread insect infestation, the more likely cause is a wrong moisture balance, or inadequate light. Check light guide on page 18, container misting, and the soil condition; make any necessary adjustments.

One plant dies, develops yellow leaves, starts drooping badly or suddenly looks generally sick. Don't bother with diagnosis, get the plant out of the terrarium and throw it away. Either it was very sick to begin with or it has developed something terrible. In such cases it is best to take no chances of the problem spreading; get rid of it.

Mealy Bugs

Tiny white cottonlike clumps form at the stem junctions or on undersides of leaves. This is a sign of the mealybugs, 1/4-inch-long insects often clumped together. Individual animals are hard to see. They like ferns, palms, dracenas, and sometimes even invade cacti. These insects suck sap which causes stunting and will eventually kill the plant. They must be stopped before they spread. Dab the infected area with rubbing alcohol on a cotton swab or give a one- or two-second burst of general purpose indoor insect spray. These measures may have to be repeated for several days. Badly infested plants are probably easier to replace than cure and should be removed.

Many brown bumps on undersides of leaves or on stems, accompanied by yellowing leaves in later stages, are indications of scale. Spray for one or two seconds with a general purpose indoor insect spray, reaching *all* infected areas.

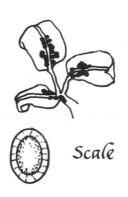

Scale

Collections of ant-sized green or brown insects, especially on new growth. These are aphids (plant lice) which suck the plant juices and stunt growth, eventually causing leaves to fall off. They are easily eradicated with a one or two-second burst of general purpose indoor insect spray.

Tiny white insects flying from plant to plant or congregated on leaves. These are white flies. Shake a plant or two to determine how widespread they are — they fly all over the place when disturbed. They have a very short incubation period, and the greatest damage comes from the larvae rather than adults. It takes persistence to wipe out white flies; the best method is a chemical-emitting pest strip hung in the container for a couple of days. For narrow-neck containers cut a small piece and suspend it by a piece of string. Recheck in one week by shaking plants.

Constantly spreading yellow or brown areas on leaves, no apparent insects. Often a sign of spider mites, or another kind of mite, which are almost impossible to see. If nothing else seems possible, assume they are the problem. You might spot tiny white saltlike granules and fine webs under leaves. At any rate, spray the undersides of leaves with an aerosol

Aphids

Spider Mites

spray containing Kelthane. In small terrariums or narrow-necks you will have to spray the whole interior and hope it gets to all areas. Wipe the spray spots off the glass with a piece of paper towel on the end of your flexible wire.

Spreading, slightly fuzzy, white, gray, or dark growths on terrarium surface or natural elements. This indicates the presence of mold, mildew, or fungus, all of which thrive in an overly humid terrarium. All are forms of fungus, and all are treated the same. If the growth is small and can be removed, or the object it is growing on removed, that is the best remedy. Leave the container open for 24 hours to dry up any you may have missed and to lower the moisture level. If the fungus reappears or persists, use a water soluble fungicide, such as Benomyl, Zineb, or Benlate. Follow the instructions carefully. Fungicides usually come in a powder form and must be mixed with water, then applied with a bulb mister or plant sprayer. Rinse the applicator thoroughly and throw away the left-over mixture. Readjust the moisture level.

In narrow-neck containers, try to remove the affected element with a mechanical grabber or terrarium tongs. If this isn't possible, direct a thin stream of fungicide at the problem area with a variable head sprayer.

This seed pod has developed mold. It was removed from the terrarium to prevent spreading

Advanced Projects

13 Animals in the Terrarium: The Vivarium

We think a vivarium, which brings animals into your miniature scene to add life and movement, is the most exciting terrarium. It is also the most demanding one because you must plan for the needs of animals as well as plants. A vivarium can provide hours of fascination, but you can't just put it on a shelf to admire. The live creatures inside need almost daily care and you must look upon this project as a continuing hobby. With proper planting and maintenance, your vivarium will be a long-term source of enjoyment and study of nature.

Establishing a home for small animals requires the same advance planning as do other large terrariums; the basic procedures and components are also the same. However, elements to meet the individual animal requirements must be added. Some people put an animal in an empty container and provide it with food and water. That is not a vivarium but a prison; food, water, and a bare room are what a criminal receives. A vivarium is a re-creation of the animals' natural habitat — plants, light, water, warmth, and food. Although they are confined, the animals live much as they would in nature without the danger of natural predators. They adjust rapidly under these circumstances and some become quite tame.

We will deal with three basic vivarium environments: tropical/aquatic, woodland, and desert. Some of the easiest animals for each

Three desert lizards appear to be having a conference.
Actually they are enjoying a noontime sunning

Sun-loving lizards cavort in this
desert vivarium. Three are easily seen.
Can you find a fourth?

environment will be suggested and their special needs listed. Animals must be carefully matched to environment; a maidenhair fern would die in a desert scene and so would a treefrog. Plants are very important to these environments, but certain animals may cause damage, so specific plants will be listed when necessary. It should be remembered that these are not for first-time terrarium builders, but are simple first-time vivarium projects.

A vivarium cannot be a closed, moisture-balanced environment. For one thing, the presence of drinking or swimming water in the container creates an overly moist atmosphere; in addition, the need to open the container for feeding and care makes a moisture balance impossible to maintain. This naturally means that the plants in a vivarium must be watered, and we will discuss plant care in the instructions for each environment.

The tropical/aquatic environment is the home of the best all-around vivarium pet, the American anole, commonly called a chameleon. Toads

will also be happy here, and if you add a swimming area you can include frogs and turtles. Hardy plants from the tropical category are used. A few hours of sun daily are advisable, but bright light will do. This vivarium provides the most animal activity of the three.

A woodland vivarium is delicate and mysterious, a home for some of nature's most fascinating creatures — newts, salamanders, frogs, and toads — living in a verdant forest of ferns, moss, and other woodland plants. Filtered sunlight is excellent, but bright or even medium light will do.

Desert vivariums are the simplest to set up and take care of. They need a sunny window, or at least some sun daily. The animals are members of the lizard family, including the popular horned toad, and the plants are from the huge cactus family, with some succulents. Planted somewhat sparsely, the desert vivarium is unexcelled for viewing the habits of your pets.

Probably your choice of a vivarium will depend on the animals you like best, so let's meet them.

Animals in the Terrarium: The Vivarium • 145

Small Vivarium Animals and Their Habits

The place to view prospective vivarium dwellers is a well-stocked pet store, a reptile specialty store, or even a tropical fish store. More than future pets will be found here — literature, containers, food, rocks, sand, and, most important of all, advice. Talk to the owner or an informed salesperson. Tell him or her your goals and interests. Most people who work in pet shops are very responsive to someone who intends to provide animals with a natural home. They will offer excellent advice on the best animals in stock and other tips.

If you find the animals you really want, pay for them and ask the owner to hold them for you until your vivarium is ready. Do not take the animals home and place them in a temporary container. They will not do well and should not be subjected to a series of different surroundings. Only when your planting is complete and in place should you add animals. It's a good idea to keep all of the animals in one vivarium

A triple-deck chameleon sandwich basks
under the light in a tropical/aquatic vivarium.
Note the two frogs in the "pool"

approximately the same size, to prevent any bullying or greediness over food. It also looks more balanced.

A brief description of the two classes of animals used in terrariums may be helpful here. A reptile is any member of the animal class Reptilia, which includes snakes, lizards, turtles, alligators, and crocodiles. Most of them have scales or bony plates. An amphibian is any member of the class Amphibia, between the fishes and the reptiles; their skins are usually soft, sometimes smooth. Frogs, toads, newts, and salamanders are amphibians, animals that spend part of their lives in water and part on land. In general, young amphibians have gills and must stay in water. Although they later develop lungs and move onto land as air breathers, they are always closely tied to water areas.

Lizards are the largest group of animals for beginning vivariums. The ones we recommend eat mealworms, small crickets, and grubs, all of which must be alive when placed in the container. This live food can be purchased at pet stores, ordered by mail, or even raised at home. Many of these lizards, especially chameleons, will eat a mealworm from the end of a wooden fondu stick, which provides extra interest in feeding your pets. Our chameleons know that when a fondu stick comes into the container it's chow time and they come running. The same trick works with flies, which you first swat and then impale on the end of the stick. The trick is to make the chameleon think the fly is alive by wiggling it slightly in front of him. These animals swallow insects whole since they cannot chew so make sure to provide small ones.

Chameleons win first place as terrarium pets, hands down. They are lively, friendly members of the lizard family who adapt quickly and

Chameleons learn to come
running when they see a
mealworm on a fondu stick
enter their home

Horned toads are really
desert lizards

constantly change color from brown to tan to light green. They are great camouflage experts and often disappear into the landscape. Chameleons can become quite tame and will eventually let you handle them, but you must work up to this very slowly. First stroke them under the chin and on the back with the fondu stick or a pencil, then your finger, until they learn to enjoy it. Then pick one up gently, for just a few seconds the first time, then for longer periods. This may take as long as a month but is fun if you want a really tame vivarium pet.

Don't ever pick up a chameleon by the tail. He will become frightened and the tail will break off. A new one will grow but it won't be as attractive as the original. Don't forget to feed him mealworms or flies on the end of a fondu stick to gain his friendship. VERY IMPORTANT: a chameleon cannot drink water from a bowl so plants must be misted daily to provide "dew." Afterward you will often see his pink tongue licking droplets from plant leaves. Many chameleons die every year because their owners do not know this habit, so be sure to include misting in your daily routine.

Males sometimes fight, so it is safest to put only one male in each container. (Males have an extra flap of skin at their throat which they inflate when courting.) You can have several females if the container is large enough, and in a large and well-planted vivarium even scraps between males will be infrequent and rarely harmful.

A tightly fitted screen cover is important as these fellows are escape artists. If one gets out, keep an eye on nearby shelves, curtains, and especially plants. He'll probably show up and be hungry! Three or four times a year chameleons shed their skin, and it's fascinating to watch the bright new skin come out from under the old. Adult length will be 6 or 7 inches, about half of which is a long, thin tail. A real winner!

Horned toads are not really toads at all, but lizards. Don't mind the ferocious look; it's just a means of protection and they won't hurt you. They are the stars of the desert vivarium and love to burrow, so provide a sand area about 3 inches deep for digging. Leaving plants in their pots and burying them to the rim is also a good idea. A warm, sunny window is best, but extra warmth can be provided by an aquarium reflector unit. For a special treat, lure some ants into a small jar with a piece of fruit and then place them in the vivarium.

Fence lizards (swifts), side-blotched lizards, whiptails, and night-lizards are all good desert dwellers. Their needs and likes are the same as those of the horned lizard. As long as they are all about the same size you can safely mix them. They usually get moisture from their food, but a small (2 to 3 inches) water bowl is welcome. Also give branches, upright rocks, and container sides a weekly misting so they can lap up moisture if they need it.

Geckos are fine vivarium subjects, but not easy to find. They are a family of lizards, and only the banded gecko is native to the U.S. but stores sometimes have others. They are mainly nocturnal, so you must provide a cave for them to hide in during daylight hours or they will constantly pace around the container and get nervous. They will come out at night, can become quite tame, and are highly recommended. Do not pick up a gecko by the tail as it breaks off very easily. Geckos are a bit fussy about temperature and the 75°-to-85° range seems best. Banded and Moorish geckos will be quite happy in a desert vivarium; for a woodland choose a Mediterranean or reef gecko. All eat mealworms. Avoid the Tokay gecko as he gets too large and bites.

Geckos seem to relish outings
with their human friends
as long as they are handled gently

Leopard frogs are fine vivarium subjects. Keep them well-fed as they can devour an animal only slightly smaller than they are

Frogs are lively, bright, easily kept vivarium subjects. Their colors range from brown through gray to green. For the tropical environment pick leopard, Florida chorus, wood frog, or the spring peeper. Tree-frogs are fine for the woodland environment, but must have a bowl of water they can crawl into. A frog has a moist, smooth skin, as opposed to a toad's which is rough and dry. All frogs need a swimming area at least two inches deep with a rock or two they can perch on. The tropical environment instructions tell how to provide this and in the woodland setting a bowl can be used. Frogs eat small crickets, mealworms, grass-hoppers, and love flies on the end of a fondu stick. They are excellent jumpers, so be careful when you have the lid open.

Toads are fatter than frogs and have a dry, warty skin. By the way, forget about getting warts from them; it hasn't happened yet. Oak toads, little green toads, and spadefoot toads are all recommended for both woodland and tropical terrariums. They grow rather fast, so buy only small ones. Toads eat mealworms, crickets, and very small earthworms, as well as flies on the end of a fondu stick. They catch insects with a flick of a tongue so fast that the insect just disappears and the frog makes a swallow. It is marvelous to watch them eating. They like to bury them-selves, so don't think one has gotten out; it's just taking a rest.

Tadpoles can be introduced into your tropical vivarium if you have adequate water for swimming — the water should be at least 4 inches deep and about one-third the area in a fifteen-gallon aquarium. Tadpoles will turn into either frogs or toads, and it's very hard to tell which from the early stages. There will be some changes almost daily, and the transi-tion from aquatic to amphibian is fascinating. Young tadpoles need Infusoria, which are tiny water organisms, for food. Fortunately pet shops now sell Infusoria tablets, so you don't need the pond water in which they grow naturally. Later, tadpoles will eat water plants, particu-

Colorful newts and salamanders
inhabit woodland vivariums. These
are California newts, whose
undersides are red-orange

larly *Elodea*, which you can get at fish supply stores, or lightly boiled pieces of lettuce. Eventually, as adults, they become insect eaters. Don't crowd tadpoles; two are enough to let you watch the change.

Turtles are lively pets commonly found in pet and dime stores. They cannot survive in a small bowl, but will be very happy in a tropical environment with a good swimming area. If you are going to have only turtles, or turtles and frogs, you could easily make the vivarium two-thirds water and only one-third land. Turtles can be rough on plants as they sometimes bury themselves and disturb the roots. Use compact, hardy plants such as sansevieria "Hahnii" or boxwood. The most popular turtle is the red-eared, also called the little green turtle. Small painted turtles are fine, too. This means the variety called painted, not those with designs painted on them. (Paint is harmful to the turtle and should be very gently scraped off with a dull knife.) Turtles for your vivariums should be 3 inches or less in diameter when you buy them, and will be slow growers. Packaged dry turtle food is the easiest way to feed them, but small bits of raw chicken or beef, mealworms, raw vegetables, and fruit will be special treats. Most of them eat in the water, so put the food there, but don't allow it to accumulate or it will foul the water.

One important caution: turtles have been found to carry a disease called salmonellosis. The ones you buy in stores should be perfectly healthy, but as a precaution wash your hands after handling them. Like most terrarium pets, they should be left in the vivarium and not played with.

Salamanders and newts are dwellers of the woodland vivarium, and should be purchased in their nonaquatic state or you must provide a fairly large swimming area for them. A newt is just one kind of salamander, and there are many kinds to choose from, some livelier than others. The Japanese red-bellied newt, California (or Western) newt, marbled salamander, and the Eastern red-spotted newt are recommended. Give them a bowl large enough for swimming, or build a pond, as in the tropical/aquatic environment. They also eat in the water, and like tubifex worms, small bits of raw fish, or shreds of beef. Older ones relish small earthworms and are great for cleaning aphids if you happen to have an infected plant. They can go many days without eating, so don't try to force-feed them. Salamanders and newts sometimes like to be secretive, so provide them with a small cave or hiding place where they can play hermit for a while. Don't worry; they'll come out when they get hungry.

We have found these the easiest and simplest animals to start with. As you get interested in vivariums you may want to move on to other lizards, tortoises, snakes, and skinks. Certain varieties make excellent subjects, although some need large containers. *All* vivarium animals take time and effort. Don't go in for this hobby in a big way until you find out if you are really interested in devoting the necessary attention. When you have gained experience with some of the animals we have listed, you can do more specialized reading on the animals you like best and their habits.

Several animals are not recommended. Some are just not good terrarium subjects. Others, like snakes, are fine for those with a special interest. We specifically advise *against*

Iguanas — O.K. when small, but grow to two feet and eat plants.

"Baby alligators" — really spectacled caimans — demanding and not friendly. They bite and are carnivorous so must be kept alone.

The atmosphere of a cool, moist forest floor has been established in this woodland vivarium

Bullfrogs — grow too large and need live food such as mice. Only for specialists.

"Purple salamanders" — which are actually orange or red — will destroy your planting with burrowing and general bad manners. Also stay away from dusky and tiger salamanders.

Northern chuckwallas — eat plants and are not very interesting anyway.

Snapping turtles — the name should tell you their story. Mud turtles and musk turtles should also be avoided.

Snakes — fine terrarium subjects, but not for a first project. Many grow quite large, need live food (not insects but animals), and special care. If you are already interested in snakes, go ahead.

Containers and Equipment

When you have decided upon an environment and the animals you want, it's time to purchase your equipment. Aquariums are by far the best containers. They come in a range of sizes and styles, are inexpensive, have full openings for ease of planting and care, and provide an undistorted view of the environment. Other containers can be used, but none have all of these qualities. In fairness to your animals, the minimum container should be ten gallons. You can safely place three or four small animals in a container of that size. A fifteen- or twenty-gallon size is much better and provides adequate room for six or seven small animals plus an opportunity to create a more roomy natural scene. Whether the aquarium is a tall or long style is up to you. Obviously a vivarium for turtles doesn't need height, but one for chameleons can use it. As always, the needs of the animals come first.

As we mentioned earlier, a vivarium cannot be a sealed environment. However, most animals, except for turtles and horned toads, will be out of the container in no time unless you provide a cover. Tropical fish stores sell framed screens for aquariums of all sizes, or you can cut your own from material purchased at a hardware store. In addition to keeping your new friends where they are supposed to be, the cover should be strong enough to support an aquarium light-reflector unit. Very few locations provide the warmth many of these animals need; if they get cold they

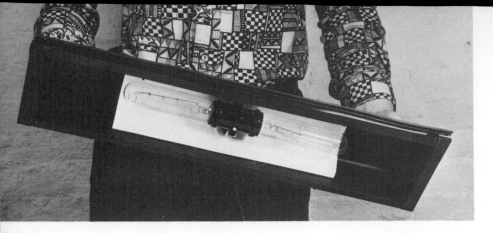

A two-bulb reflector unit made
by O'Dell Manufacturing provides
needed warmth and light

bury themselves or hibernate, which is not what you want at all. These units are readily available at tropical fish stores, not costly, and provide heat for the animals and an illuminated view of your scene during the day and through the evening. Be sure to get a unit that uses incandescent bulbs; fluorescent fixtures do not provide sufficient heat. Of course, if your location provides the proper temperature and you want only light, the fluorescents are fine.

To help keep heat and moisture in, we cut a piece of plastic sheeting, such as that used for paint drop cloths, to rest on the cover and fit around the reflector unit. This is easily removed for feeding or opening the lid. It should not totally seal the vivarium because the humidity would become too high, especially in the desert environment.

Temperature is very important to vivariums, much more so than to other terrariums, for animals are less tolerant of extremes than plants. Here is a chart of preferred temperature ranges and light conditions:

Environment	Day Temperature	Night Temperature	Light
Tropical/aquatic	75° to 85°	65° to 75°	Some sun, bright light
Woodland	65° to 75°	60° to 70°	Bright or medium light Filtered sun good
Desert	80° to 90°	65° to 80°	Full sun, bright light

It is a good idea to place a small thermometer in the vivarium occasionally to see if you are providing the proper amount of warmth or coolness.

A very handy piece of equipment to add is a timer that automatically turns the lights on and off. This relieves you of having to do it and provides the same hours of warmth and light each day. If you go away for a few days it will assure you that your animals are warm and cozy at home. Do not leave the lights on continuously; both the plants and animals like a resting period of about eight hours nightly.

Vivarium Shopping List

By now you should be familiar with our shopping list. Many of the planting needs you probably have on hand.

Container — a ten- to twenty-gallon aquarium is best

Cover — aquarium cover from fish store or heavyweight, small-weave screen

Aquarium reflector, bulbs, and (optional) timer

Planting elements — gravel, charcoal, soil separator, soil mix components according to environment

Tools — scissors, mixing bowl, large spoon, tamper

Water container — small bowl for desert, medium bowl for woodland, large bowl or piece of glass and silicone sealer for tropical/aquatic

Food dish — can be quite small, but must be 1 inch deep. Otherwise mealworms may escape and become inhabitants of your scene

Plants — according to environment, see planting instructions for suggestions

Bulb sprayer or plant mister — for initial and later watering

Animals — only after vivarium is completed

Food — from same source as animals

Planting Instructions

Although the design and planting procedures for vivariums are very similar to those for any other large terrarium, certain modifications must be made for the animals' needs. Placement of food and water containers and special habits such as burrowing or climbing will influence your design. In general, we keep the plants toward the rear and sides, leaving the foreground rather open. This is an excellent place to sink the food dish so your animals will be in full view at dinnertime.

Tropical/aquatic. Same planting procedure as given in chapter 11. The animals in this terrarium will be chameleons, frogs, toads, and turtles. Chameleons are great climbers and will spend most of their time perched on plants or small branches. Be sure to have a branch under the light source so they can "sun" themselves. Toads need only a small bowl of water; frogs and turtles need a swimming area.

To create a miniature pond in your vivarium you need a piece of glass cut exactly to the width of the container and about 5 inches high, plus a tube of rubber-based aquarium sealer from a tropical fish or hardware store. Place the glass separator in position, allowing one-third to one-half water space for frogs and turtles, two-thirds water for turtles alone. Support the glass at about a 35° angle with two boxes, a beanbag, or almost anything else you have on hand. (See photo.) Use the aquarium sealer to fasten the glass in place. The instructions will probably say that it must dry for forty-eight hours. To be on the safe side, let it sit twenty-four hours, then give it a light second coat and let it sit another forty-eight hours. Be sure to get all the points where the glass wall joins the container well sealed, sides and bottom. It is *essential* that you test the waterproof quality of your partition before any planting begins. If water leaks through and into the "dry" side it will saturate the soil and kill the plants. Fill the pond with water and let it sit for a day. Check for leaks and reseal if necessary. Then you are ready to plant.

Cover the bottom of the pond with gravel, sloping it up to where it joins the dry part of your vivarium. Be sure to add some rocks for perching. Do not add water until the completed project is in place, to cut down on moving weight and avoid sloshing water all over.

A substitute pond may be made from a slant-sided bowl so long as it

A fifteen-gallon Ambassador aquarium is turned into a tropical/aquatic vivarium by the addition of a glass partition to separate water and land areas

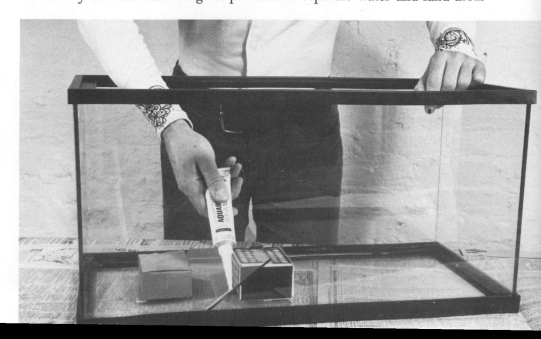

provides room for real swimming, not just soaking. Be sure that there are rocks for the animals to crawl on. Turtles cannot get out of the bowl if the sides are slippery unless climbing rocks are provided.

Select your plants from the hardy tropical category. Remember that chameleons will climb on them, but these animals are very light and only a very spindly one would be damaged. Especially good plants are:

Chinese Evergreen	Philodendron	Peperomia
Dracaena	Parlor Palm	Sansevieria "Hahnii"
English Ivy	Pothos	

Plants should be given a light misting daily. This is especially important if you have chameleons as it provides their only source of drinking water and insures the plants' health at the same time. A thorough watering should be given once a week and increased to twice a week during warmer months.

A food bowl should be provided to hold mealworms. Turtles must be fed in the water. For full feeding information, check listing for the animals you choose.

Woodland. Animals will be toads, some frogs, salamanders, and newts. A bowl for swimming is needed by all but the toads. Be sure to put a few rocks in the bowl so the salamanders and newts can crawl out if the bowl has steep or slippery sides. A ceramic bowl in a natural dark color works best, but glass or plastic can be used and blended in by the use of gravel.

Plastic sheeting over the cover is excellent for increasing the humidity. Since this is the coolest of the three environments, you may not need a reflector unit for warmth. Check the temperature in the planned location, and remember that the animals will bury themselves if the vivarium

Planting of the "dry" area is done with tropical plants. The "pond" will be filled when the vivarium is in position

An overall view of a woodland terrarium in a fifteen-gallon tank by O'Dell, inhabited by salamanders, newts, and treefrogs

becomes too cold. If you don't use a light, a solid glass cover ³⁄₁₆ inch thick can be used, propped up at the corners to allow excess moisture to escape. Mist the plants daily and water well once a week, twice a week in warm weather. Check the soil by sticking a finger in it to test dryness before watering. It should be kept rather evenly moist, but not soggy.

Follow the general planting instructions given in chapter 11, but remember to do some good banking here. There should be a more graceful feeling than in the other vivariums; don't overplant or your animals will be hard to see. Salamanders and newts need a hiding cave, which you can make from a few rocks. Select plants from the woodland list. Since you won't have lizards to crawl on them, you can use any you like. Ferns will be fine as long as you keep up your misting program. Ground covers such as partridgeberry and pellionia are good, and moss can be used extensively.

Frogs and toads need a feeding dish; salamanders and newts will use it for earthworms and mealworms but will eat tubifex worms in the water.

Desert. Follow the general planting procedure in chapter 8. All of your animals will be desert lizards, most of which like to burrow. Provide a sand area 3 inches deep at the front or one end of the planting for this purpose. Use a desert soil mix for the planting area, but do not add perlite as it makes the soil mix very light and if the animals burrow in it they may upset the plants. You may even want to leave the plants in their pots and fill the entire container with sand. That's O.K., but don't forget the gravel, charcoal, and soil separator. The colored-layer effect may or may not be disturbed by burrowing, but a modified version is worth a try.

This vivarium will almost always need the extra warmth of a two-bulb reflector unit. Put a sturdy rock, plant, or branch under the lights so the animals can bask in its warmth. Also provide a sheltered spot *out* of the sun where the animals can escape heat.

Any and all cacti will do well, but some of the taller, spindly types can topple over when perched on. Don't worry about the spines; these guys scamper right up and sit down on most cacti. Succulents are susceptible to damage from being climbed over, so use sturdy types such as jade plant and sempervivum; avoid weak stems.

Follow general desert terrarium maintenance, except that the cooler winter temperatures must be omitted or your animals will hide. As long as the plants have a dry winter this will cause no harm, although they probably won't flower. Feed the animals three times a week with enough mealworms in a bowl to last a day. Small crickets can just be turned loose in the vivarium and will be searched out by your pets. A bowl of water big enough for them to crawl into should be provided. Mist some rocks, branches, or container walls to provide "dew" for drinking or let water run over the plants, particularly succulents, when watering. Check individual animal descriptions for further care.

14 Terrariums Under Artificial Lights

A whole new world opened to indoor gardeners with the widespread availability and lower prices of lights for growing plants indoors. These lights make it possible for you to have a terrarium in any room or location; even the darkest corner of your basement can house a prospering terrarium. Lights can be used to bring tropical and woodland plantings to interior offices, dim hallways, or even inside a closet, as one apartment-dweller friend of ours does.

There are three important ways you can use artificial light for terrariums:

1. As a secondary source of light where there is some, but not enough, natural light.

2. As a total source of light in a location where there is insufficient or no natural light.

3. As a means of bringing flowering plants into fullest bloom.

(Growing desert plants under lights is a project for specialists and will not be covered.)

With the use of an artificial light fixture you can put a terrarium anywhere you want, as long as the temperature range is within that of a normal living area. You must decide, however, whether you need total light or just secondary light to augment natural sources. As a guide, secondary light is needed if the location receives only four hours of good

A whole collection of terrariums
can be lighted by a mercury vapor bulb,
with no natural light needed

The simplest way
to provide secondary
light is with an
ordinary table lamp

reading light a day. Total light is needed if natural sources provide less than four hours of good reading light a day. Here's another way to judge: any spot more than 15 feet from a sunny window or 10 feet away from a bright-light window will need artificial light — secondary if the natural light is high throughout the year, and total if natural light is low. Tropical plants generally like a little more light than woodland plants, but some are also tolerant of low light so the plants you choose will also have some bearing on the extra light you need.

Artificial Light as a Secondary Light Source

The simplest way to provide additional light to supplement natural daylight is an ordinary 60- to 100-watt light bulb in a table, floor, or hanging lamp, left on six or more hours a day. The bulb should be from 8 to 12 inches above the terrarium or highest plant and shine directly down onto it. This light source is fine for a terrarium in the borderline area between almost, but not quite enough, light. It can extend your use of terrariums to many living areas that can't completely support a terrarium but where you don't want to put a special fixture.

The second possibility is the use of either a shelf-mounted or free-standing fluorescent unit, which provides the coolest and most economical means of reproducing natural light. A shelf unit allows you to use longer bulbs; the addition of a front valance hides the fixture and creates a built-in appearance.

Garden centers, plant stores, hardware, and electrical supply stores carry both the fixtures and the bulbs, which are available in 18-inch, 24-inch, 36-inch, and 48-inch sizes. The length, of course, is determined by the location you have chosen. Several kinds of bulbs specially formulated for plant growing are on the market. Our choice is the "full (or wide) spectrum bulb," which produces most of the growing rays of natural light. We use either the Vita-Lite or Natur-escent bulbs by Duro-Test. A less expensive choice is a combination of one "cool white" and one "warm white" fluorescent bulb. These are general-purpose bulbs not formulated for plant growing, but can be used as a substitute although the "full spectrum" are preferred.

An undershelf fluorescent unit makes terrarium growing possible even in an unlikely location such as this

"Grow" bulbs by Duralite
provide a floodlight effect and
are a fine source of secondary
light for groups of terrariums

Shelf fixtures are easily mounted with a few screws under any wooden surface, such as a bookcase or kitchen cabinet. A two-bulb fixture is best for most spots, but a single unit will be sufficient where only slight supplemental light is needed.

Free-standing units are mostly available in 18-inch and 24-inch sizes. Design tends to be more practical than decorative, but is constantly being improved. Most have a handy height-adjustment feature that allows you to vary the distance between your container and the bulbs. They also have the advantage of being completely portable and can be used where there is no overhanging support for a built-in unit. They come with and without bulbs, so check carefully on the type of bulb you are getting if it is a package deal.

A light reflector is a very important part of a fluorescent unit. Most shelf units come equipped with a white reflector; this greatly increases the amount of light the plants receive. Always try to buy a unit with a reflector to gain maximum benefit from your fluorescent unit. Free-standing units almost always come with a light reflector that is part of the assembly.

In either case the bulbs should be 6 to 10 inches above the container or the top of the tallest plant. As a secondary light they should be used six to seven hours a day, during the daylight or early evening hours. Make sure the terrarium receives at least eight hours of darkness and rest at night.

The third method of providing secondary light is from one of the widely distributed incandescent "grow" or "plant" bulbs. They will floodlight an area about 4 feet in diameter with a light that has been engineered to provide the plants with vital rays. The most popular sizes are 75 and 150 watts. These bulbs should be mounted in reflector units, which come in a variety of styles, from utilitarian clamp-on to expensive, futuristic designs. The bulbs are cone-shaped with a diameter of 4 or 5½ inches, so make sure that your reflector unit can accommodate a bulb that size. Place a 150-watt bulb 4 feet away from the terrarium location; a 75-watt bulb should be 3 feet away. The same time span of seven to eight hours of light per day should be used. When lighted, these bulbs tend to break if any moisture gets on them, so be careful if you are misting or watering any plants.

Timers are extremely helpful to insure a consistent amount of light every day and are well worth their cost to free you from turning your lights on and off. We recommend them for all artificial light set-ups.

Artificial Light as a Total Light Source

Wherever natural light is very inadequate or nonexistent, your plants will be entirely dependent upon artificial lights, and you must be more exact in your use of them. Most important is that you provide adequate intensity and duration of light. We recommend either the two-bulb

Overhead office lighting is sufficient for terrariums in many buildings

These terrariums receive no natural light, yet thrive under
a two-bulb fluorescent unit

fluorescent unit or a self-ballasted mercury vapor bulb, and always the
use of a timer.

Fluorescent units can be in a shelf or free-standing style, with either
two full or wide spectrum bulbs, or a "cool white" and "warm white"
combination. These are the same lights used for secondary lighting, but
they are left on from twelve to fourteen hours daily. Light duration can
be reduced if growth becomes too rapid.

Self-ballasted mercury vapor bulbs offer a second way to grow terrariums where natural light is inadequate. They can also be used as a
secondary light source, but the price is a little high and other units will
do a fine job. These bulbs throw a circle of excellent light over an area
about 6 feet in diameter when placed 5 to 7 feet away from a terrarium.

They come in 160- and 250-watt sizes and must be mounted in a reflector fixture with a ceramic socket because they generate a fair amount of heat. Do not place them any closer to the plants than 5 feet and set the timer for twelve to fourteen hours of light daily. Many mercury vapor bulbs are offered; we prefer Jewel Electric's Super-Lumen bulb, available at large garden centers, plant stores, or large electrical supply stores. These bulbs are best used to flood a really dramatic terrarium collection on shelves. With well-balanced terrariums, lights, and a timer you can spend three weeks on vacation and never have to worry about your plants.

Artificial lights are usually necessary for an impressive flowering plant display in a terrarium. Blooms will occur only in a *very* bright location without them, and not year round. With lights you can have blooms in any location, throughout the year. A two-bulb fluorescent unit is always recommended. The timer should be set for eight to ten hours as a supplemental source, and twelve to fourteen hours for a total light source, placed 6 to 8 inches above the container or tallest plant.

The mercury vapor bulb must be mounted in a ceramic socket fixture

15 Flowering Plants

The use of flowering plants brings additional color and many exciting new plants into your miniature scenes. They must be tended a little more carefully than foliage plants, and *extremely* bright light locations or artificial light is necessary for them to achieve fullest bloom. But you'll discover nothing quite matches them for inspiring "oh's" and "ah's" when the blossoms appear.

The flowering plants in this chapter will thrive under tropical terrarium conditions. Some of them are also at home in woodland plantings. We like to combine blooming plants with background and ground-cover plants from the foliage group, giving the flowers center stage in the setting. Although a blooming terrarium must be ventilated occasionally or left slightly open the plants will still receive a high degree of humidity and the other improved growing conditions of a closed environment. If you combine a terrarium atmosphere with fluorescent lights, your plants will produce a quality and quantity of blossoms unattainable under other conditions. In fact, we strongly recommend the use of artificial lights to achieve real success with blooming plants.

The style of container you select for a flowering plant terrarium should be based on the plants you choose and the feeling you want to create. Maintenance will be greatly simplified if you select a container with an opening wide enough for your hand. One spectacular miniature African

169

A small space at the end of a breakfast table brings
a blooming garden every morning

violet in full bloom is gratifying enough for many people; others prefer an aquarium tank with many plants. You can also use the terrarium as a greenhouse or nursery, leaving the plants in their pots and concentrating on the individual plants instead of a total landscaped effect. For a doubly effective planting, use a mirror-backed aquarium. In addition to reflecting your plants, the mirror will act to increase the light they receive for even healthier growth.

How you want to use flowering plants in a terrarium will probably be determined by the plants you want to grow. Here are the ones we recommend:

African Violet. *Saintpaulia* is probably the most popular indoor flowering plant in the U.S. Miniature varieties should be used in terrariums as the standards become too large. Colors range through purple, blue, pink,

Metaframe's twenty-gallon aquarium is ideal for a basement blooming-plant nursery. A convenient sliding top provides humidity control

Miniature African violet, wax begonia, episcia

and white, with both single and double flowers. African violets enjoy the high terrarium humidity, but a *thorough* weekly airing is essential. Try a single specimen in a globe with creeping pilea or selaginella around the perimeter for a real show-stopper.

Begonia. An extremely large genus of plants with several varieties well-suited to terrariums. Be sure to stick with the small ones as they really take off in a terrarium. The easiest to grow is the wax begonia, *B. semperflorens*, which produces a brilliant show of red, pink, or white flowers. It may drop leaves in an overly moist terrarium, so a slight opening or a half-hour airing out every few days is helpful. Other good varieties are *B. boweri* (miniature eyelash), *B. prismatocarpa*, *B. richardsiana*, *B. subnummularifolia*, *B. versicolor* (fairy carpet), and *B. weltonensis* (mapleleaf). These are by no means all the begonias that can be grown in terrariums and you should experiment with any small ones you like, or ask for suggestions from your plant source.

Crossandra. A year-round bloomer with orange flowers, dark green, shiny leaves, and a liking for terrarium conditions. The flower spikes may grow 12 inches tall, so use a large container or pinch the plant back to keep it compact and bushy. Adaptable for woodland environments.

Episcia. Often called flame violet; all small ones are excellent terrarium plants. The flowers come in white, pink, yellow, red, orange, and lavender, and they have attractive variegated foliage to boot. Pinching back can be useful to keep them terrarium size. Particularly good varieties are *E. cupreata*, *E. lilacina*, and *E. punctata*.

Gloxinera, orchid, sinningia

Gloxinera. A hybrid relative of the popular gloxinia that is excellent in the foreground. Miniature varieties are from 3 to 6 inches high and have flowers in shades of pink to lavender blue. After flowering, the foliage will disappear, but the bulb (corm) will resprout in a few months and a whole new flowering cycle will begin. Some recommended varieties are: cupid doll, little imp, pink flare, pink imp, pink petite, and tinkerbell.

Orchid. Although these exotic and beautiful plants are ideally suited to terrariums, orchid growing calls for very different cultural procedures from those we have discussed, and getting them to bloom requires a fair amount (sometimes a great deal) of care. We could not begin to cover the growing of orchids in a single chapter; many books have been written on the subject. If you have experience with orchids or want to try them, the use of a large aquarium case is recommended, but specialized reading on the types of orchids you can grow and their needs should be done first.

Sinningia. A marvelous miniature relative of the florist's gloxinia that will bloom through the year. It has trumpet-shaped flowers in shades of red, pink, purple, and white, some with dark or spotted throats. *S. pusilla* and *S. concinna* are the smallest of all. Other varieties that are recommended are: bright eyes, cindy, doll baby, freckles, poupée, white sprite, wood nymph, and snow flake.

Smithiantha. Often called temple bells. Most send up a single flower stalk; the colors are whites, reds, oranges, and yellows. The plant goes dormant after blooming but will resprout in a few months, so remember where it is. Some plants will grow to about 12 inches high, but any with the word "little" in its name will stay about half that size.

Streptocarpus. Most of the better known varieties of this plant are too large for terrariums, but some wonderful small ones are available. Look for *S. saxorum*, any variety with the word "nymph" in its name, or a miniature. All of these are compact, lend themselves to free flowering, and can also be used in woodland terrariums.

While all of the plants on this list will bloom in very bright natural light, they will really perform much better with the addition of artificial lighting. Then you are assured of perfect growing conditions every day — rainy weather, shortened winter days, and less than ideal locations do not affect them. If you are interested enough to delve into blooming plants, do it all the way and use a two-bulb fluorescent unit above them. The wealth of blooms your plants will produce will be ample recompense for the extra effort and expense.

Planting and Maintenance

The planting procedures for blooming plants are generally the same as those for other terrariums. If you add blooming plants to terrariums that contain tropical or woodland foliage plants, you can follow the general recommendations for those environments.

If your terrarium has only blooming plants, use a tropical soil mix. The same subsurface elements and steps are used. The initial watering is also the same.

After your flowering plant terrarium is in its permanent location, watch the moisture balance and make corrections if necessary in the usual way; be very careful to correct heavy misting as that is detrimental to these plants. *In addition, flowering plants should be given a thorough airing at least once a week.* Open the cover about one quarter of the way and leave it open for two or three hours. The terrarium can then be closed and you can see how well the moisture balance re-establishes itself.

Obviously this step is going to create a need for additional water. You may want to add a little after each airing, or in a day or two to see how much is needed. An alternate method is to leave the lid slightly open and check the misting level every few days.

Blooming plants under lights need some fertilizing to maintain their continued vigor. Use a water soluble, organic fertilizer mixed to *one-fourth* the strength recommended on the label. Use a 5-10-10 organic fertilizer, and be very careful not to exceed one-fourth the recommended strength. Apply fertilizer with a bulb sprayer to the area around the plant once every three months; do not spray fertilizer water on leaves.

The flowering plants listed above will do best within a daytime temperature range of 65° to 75°, with a 10° drop at night. Begonias and streptocarpus will appreciate a nightime drop to 55°.

To produce really healthy, compact blooming plants, some specimens, especially begonias and espiscias, will need a bit of pinching back. It takes a great deal of will power to pinch back a plant that is growing like crazy and just on the verge of blooming, so do it before the plant reaches this stage. You don't want to end up with a straggly, elongated plant with a few blooms at the top. The key to avoiding this is a keen eye and frequent observation. Look at the plants as they grow and watch their lines. When a portion of the plant starts to get out of bounds, it must be pinched back to maintain a bushy shape. This is a technique you will learn with experience. Place the stems of the pinched-off segments in a small pot of vermiculite and place them in a "greenhouse" terrarium to start new plants.

Removing all dead blooms is another very important maintenance procedure. Do not just pull off the faded flower; cut or pinch off the entire

This wax begonia is on the way to becoming elongated and spindly. The re-shaped plant will be more compact and produce more flowers

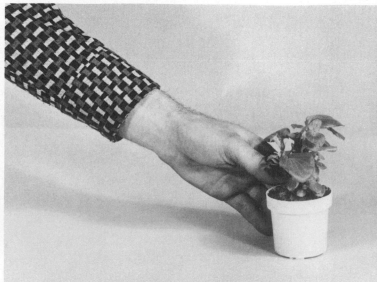

A small container such as this is perfect for displaying one miniature blooming plant

Raising orchids is a rewarding, though specialized, terrarium project

A blooming
sinningia highlights
a tropical planting

supporting stem or stalk to remove the seed-producing elements that are
left when the flowering is finished (see diagram).

The plants recommended here are by no means the only flowering
plants that can be grown in terrariums, but they are the ones we consider
best for initial planting. After you have succeeded with them you may
want to try others, or work with different combinations and other containers. Experimenting with new ideas is part of the fun of being an
advanced terrarium planter.

a. Wrong way to remove a faded
blossom. *b.* Correct way, with all
reproductive elements removed

16 Carnivorous-Plant Terrariums

A carnivorous-plant terrarium will bring you into contact with some of nature's strangest creations. These incredible plants lure, trap, and digest insects to obtain needed chemicals and nutrition. They are quite unlike any of the other plants discussed in this book and require a separate terrarium with conditions suited to their needs.

Carnivorous, or insectivorous, plants attract insects by odor, color, or a combination of the two. Once attracted, the insect is trapped as a part of the plant closes around it, or caught by sticky hairlike growths, or lured into a "one-way" passage. The insect is then digested by secretion or other means and the needed elements are absorbed by the plant. Many of these are excellent terrarium subjects. Let's meet a few.

Plants that drown their victims are called pitcher plants. They have tubular or pitcherlike leaves that hold water and downward-pointing, slippery hairs that allow the insect to go into the plant but not out. The insect cannot gain a foothold or escape and moves further and further downward until it reaches the reservoir of water inside the "pitcher." There it drowns and begins to decay, aided by secretions from the plant. The plant then absorbs needed elements from the water. By the way, the pitchers are filled with water drawn up from the growing medium, not from falling rain or dew.

Six varieties of insect-eating plants inhabit this terrarium. Artificial lights have produced the flower buds seen on several species

The most widely available pitcher plants are members of the *Sarracenia* genus and *Darlingtonia californica*, commonly called the cobra lily or cobra plant. All of these are recommended for your terrarium, although a few grow quite tall and need a container 20 inches high.

A second method of trapping insects is a sticky secretion, used by the sundews, *Drosera*, and the butterworts, *Pinguicula*. Sundew leaves have small, reddish hairs tipped with tiny drops of glistening "dew" that give off an odor attractive to insects, but are also fatally sticky. The insect is drawn to the plant by the perfume, investigates the source, and is soon trapped by the "dew." Struggling only further enmeshes the insect until it is completely trapped, surrounded, and fed upon. When the feeding is over, the hairs open and the insect skeleton can be brushed away.

Butterworts are closely related to the sundews but have a sticky substance at the end of each leaf. When an insect is trapped the leaf margin rolls around it, completely surrounding it for feeding purposes. Both of these plants are small, usually 1 or 2 inches in diameter, though butterworts can be double that size.

A third method of trapping insects is used by the most popular and well known carnivorous plant, the Venus flytrap, *Dionaea muscipula*. At the tip of each leaf this plant develops a remarkable trap consisting of two lobes. Around the outside edges of the lobes are sharp, inward-curved spines; inside the lobes are three (sometimes four) small black bristles. Insects are attracted to the plant by its odor and when they wander far enough into a trap to touch one of the inside hairs the trap closes. The spines interlock to form a tiny prison, and the insect is slowly dissolved over a period lasting a week or more. The trap then opens and is ready for a new victim. After digesting two or three insects the traps will turn dark and drop off, but new leaves with new traps will constantly be put forth.

Insect-eating plants are available at many garden centers or can be ordered by mail from the sources listed at the end of this book. They are usually sold or shipped in moisture-proof plastic bags or containers, which also contain directions for growing the specific plant you have

Venus flytrap

Sundew

Yellow-hooded pitcher plant

A cobra lily in a dome terrarium by Christen.
It is excellent for displaying one plant

purchased. Save these directions and follow them in conjunction with the general carnivorous plant instructions in this chapter.

Narrow-neck bottles are obviously not suitable for insectivorous plants but almost any other container will do, depending on the quantity and size of the plants you want. Some pitcher plants require a container that is 20 inches high; a dome with a single specimen is dramatic. A single Venus flytrap in a small globe is always an attention-getter. If you want to grow several different varieties, an aquarium works best. In any case, make sure you can either reach inside the container or open the lid easily for feeding purposes.

All carnivorous-plant terrariums need the usual 1- to 2-inch layer of gravel for drainage, sprinkled with charcoal at the rate of one tablespoon per cup of drainage. A soil separator cut to size should be placed over this. There are two possible growing mediums, both used successfully. The first is a 1- to 2-inch layer of acid soil mix (half sterilized potting soil and half peat moss) topped by an equal amount of either live or dried sphagnum moss. The other is long-fibered sphagnum only, without any soil mix. In either case don't use artificially colored sphagnum.

The plants should be gently nestled into the sphagnum, with their roots reaching down into the soil mix if you are using one. Push sphagnum moss around the roots so that there is good contact, but don't pack it tightly. Plants purchased in the fall and winter are often in a dormant stage and look somewhat lifeless. When planted and given good light, they should show new growth within a month. Don't worry if an occasional leaf turns brown and drops off. This is a natural occurrence and you can cut it off when it turns or remove it after it falls.

Since these plants are bog dwellers and love humidity, you can give them a very heavy misting. They will be happier if you use distilled water, spring water, melted snow, or rainwater. If you do use treated tap water, allow it to sit a day to let the chlorine escape and sediment settle.

Carnivorous terrariums need bright light, and a two-bulb fluorescent unit is advised. The bulbs should be 6 to 8 inches above the container and should be left on twelve to fourteen hours daily if total light is needed, or eight hours for supplemental use. This will promote excellent growth and vigorous, hungry plants.

Temperature should be in the 65°-to-75° range, with a 10° drop at night. They do not like cold weather and should not be subjected to temperatures below 50°. Normal misting guidelines apply to carnivorous terrariums, but slightly heavier than normal condensation is beneficial.

A single Venus flytrap terrarium.
A live fly placed inside will be
trapped and eaten by the plant

The most important and most interesting part of carnivorous terrariums is the feeding of the plants. First of all, do not give them plant food or fertilizer; it is not a substitute for insects and can be harmful. During the warmer months you should have no trouble obtaining ants, flies, small crickets, gnats, and other insects for your plants. Put out a jar with a piece of fruit, meat, or other food that will attract them. Come back in an hour or so and clap on the lid. Then put the jar or the insects into your terrarium. Replace the terrarium cover and sit back to watch the show. The show, however, may not be instantaneous. You must be patient and wait for the insects to be drawn to the plants. It may take a while for them to be attracted, but they will be and you will be able to see your plants in action.

You may choose to place individual insects on the plants, perhaps with a pair of tweezers. They are best given whole and alive, since their struggles activate the plant. If necessary, you can cut them into smaller portions and place them in the correct place for the plant to absorb them.

Do not try to feed newly planted specimens. Wait until they have established themselves and show some new growth.

During the months that live insects are not available you should try to get fruit flies, very small mealworms, or young crickets from a pet store. You may also try very small pieces of lean meat dropped into the proper location, such as the lobes of a Venus flytrap. Feed sparingly with this method.

The fascination of carnivorous plants is in their strange shapes and their trapping and eating procedures. They can become almost like pets, with a need to be fed and cared for. As with pets, it is important that they have adequate water and not be overfed. In return they will perform a truly unique array of insect-eating tricks.

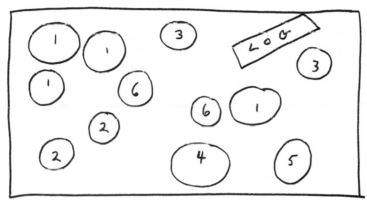

1. Cobra lily
2. Min. Huntsman's Horns
3. Northern Pitcher Plant
4. Sundews
5. Butterworts
6. Parrot Pitcher Plant

Diagram of the large insectivorous terrarium on page 178. Such a diagram should be made for any terrarium with different species

Just for Fun

17 Terrarium Ideas for Youngsters

We believe that terrariums should be made and enjoyed by people of all ages. Many of the terrariums in this book are perfect for children and teenagers, who will find them an excellent way of watching nature in operation.

Of the four projects we discuss in this chapter, the first three can be undertaken even by very young children, although they should have some help; older ones can handle them alone. The first part of each one should be a shopping trip to obtain any materials not on hand. The second part of each project is the actual assembly. Be sure to find a place where your budding terrarium gardener can work for an hour or so without being disturbed or in anyone's way. Outside is best, for it minimizes clean-up needs; a garage, basement, or playroom is fine if a layer of papers is laid down first. Two youngsters working together will usually have more fun, and some procedures work better with four hands than two.

Older or science-minded children will probably enjoy reading the first chapter to understand how terrariums came into existence and how they work. Then the chapter pertaining to the specific terrarium project they have selected should be read. The four projects recommended are good starting places for youngsters, and then any of the other terrariums we describe can be used as follow-up undertakings.

This tropical terrarium in a cookie jar from
Anchor Hocking took 45 minutes to assemble and
will be a source of enjoyment for months to come

A Closed Tropical Terrarium

This project is a wonderful way to get children interested in terrariums. It is easily constructed by following the instructions for the first-time terrarium, which are simple and foolproof; for older children more emphasis can be placed on design and the use of surface elements.

It's a good idea to select a container with an opening large enough for the child to get both hands inside. The cookie jar seen in the photograph is a perfect size. Prepackaged terrarium soil mix could be used, but mixing one's own is more interesting and provides valuable indoor gardening experience. Remember that plants should be in 2-inch pots, or even smaller. Especially recommended for their hardiness are:

Arrowhead	Boxwood	Chinese Evergreen
English Ivy	Euonymus	Maranta
Peperomia	Philodendron	Podocarpus
Pothos	Sansevieria "Hahnii'	

Several of these, such as philodendron, will soon show new growth and provide visual results of success. The maranta's habit of folding its leaves at night always appeals to children.

If your children are of an age that needs a little help, by all means provide it, but don't be surprised if they work things out by themselves and invent some of their own rules. In testing this project with eight-to-ten-year-olds we found they quickly figured out ways to do things that were not described but worked very well. Be prepared to answer ques-

a. Make sure that *all* materials are on hand before youngsters start to work. *b.* Cutting the soil separator works well this way. *c.* A salt shaker to apply water assures even distribution

tions and explain why things are done the way they are, such as the use of different elements in a soil mix, and why overwatering will kill the plants.

Keep an eye out for the over-eager planter who might miss a step; make sure he finishes each step completely and then reads through the next one before starting on it. Surface elements should be kept to rocks and pebbles to cut down on the chance of mold or insects. Keeping water on the spare side is much better than applying too much.

Most children will enjoy this planting so much they will want to do more. Let them plant some as gifts for grandparents, aunts, uncles, and other relatives, who will treasure these works. Be sure to have them planted at least two weeks in advance to adjust the moisture balance.

To remove a plant from its pot, position fingers this way, turn it over, and give bottom a good thump with the bowl of a spoon

An Open Cactus Garden

Even very young children seem to know that a cactus is different from other plants. Making a small windowsill cactus garden is easy for youngsters, once they learn how to deal with the spines. Success is assured if a sunny location and very light watering are stressed from the beginning.

When shopping for plants be sure to allow the builder to pick out a range of unusual plants, such as old man cactus with its woolly "hair" or a brightly colored grafted cactus for accent. The container can be made of plastic, ceramic, or glass; a depth of around 3 inches and a diameter of about 7 inches is fine. Other needed materials as well as the planting procedure are given in the cacti and succulents chapter. Be sure to advise the use of leather gloves for handling prickly specimens.

Younger children may need a bit of help in removing the plants from the pots and positioning them, but otherwise planting is easy. It's especially helpful to have two people work on this planting so one can hold plants in position while the other one tamps them in.

This terrarium can be placed outside in the summer, as long as it does not get soaked by rain. Since it has no drainage holes, this would be fatal. A porch where it would receive sun but be protected from rain is ideal. In such a location water could be applied twice a week during the really hot months.

a. Leather gloves make cactus handling easy.
b. One person should steady plant while another places soil mix and tamps. *c.* A very light watering with a bulb sprayer completes the desert terrarium. The sprayer will also be used for future waterings

Two proud and happy youngsters with their desert terrarium

Insect–Eating Terrariums

Children are fascinated by these plants, and a Venus flytrap is great for younger ones. Teen-agers may want to try a larger terrarium with a variety of specimens. Full instructions for these terrariums are given in the chapter devoted to carnivorous plants, but the larger size should not be tried without some experience.

Children interested in botany should be encouraged to keep a record of the plants' eating habits, such as how long it takes a lobe to reopen after trapping a fly. In some of the pitcher plants you can see the insects being trapped and also floating in the pitcher's water. The investment in a two-bulb fluorescent unit will allow this terrarium to be placed anywhere, such as a bookshelf or basement, where it can provide hours of interest.

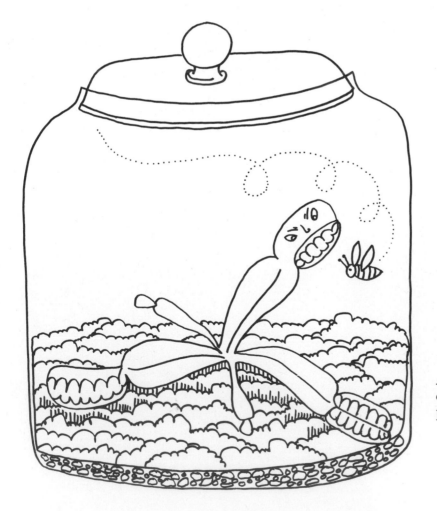

A single Venus flytrap in a cookie jar makes an excellent project for youngsters

Chameleons are among
the best and liveliest
vivarium animals
for children

Vivariums

The vivarium is a project only for the teen-ager who will really stick with it. A passing interest in setting one up without the ability to follow through with feeding and care will result in the death of the animals. If it becomes obvious that the vivarium is not going to be cared for, it's better to return the animals to the pet store or free them in a suitable location than to let them languish.

A desert vivarium is easier to take care of than a tropical or woodland setting. Plant maintenance is low, and mealworms plus a bowl of water will keep desert lizards happy. Small toads in a tropical vivarium are also easy pets. Chameleons, with their knack of eating insects off a wooden fondu stick, are the most entertaining pet, but remember that daily misting is necessary as they do not drink water from a bowl. Frogs need a swimming area, and a tadpole can be added to show the change from water dweller to air breather.

Small children have always enjoyed turtles, but the possibility of salmonellosis should be mentioned, and handling them should be forbidden.

All vivariums provide a close-up look at the way animals live and the interaction of plant and animal life. They are sure to attract those who have an interest in biology, zoology, or ecology. There is no better way for a youngster to develop these interests than by having the experience of caring for and observing animals in his own home.

Buffet ready for serving, with six newly-made terrariums as decoration

18 A Terrarium Planting Party

Once you have become an established terrarium builder, you will find that you are constantly asked three questions:

"How did you do it?"

"How can I do it?"

"Would you make one for me?"

To answer all of these questions and have fun at the same time, why not give a terrarium-planting party? We gave one to celebrate the conclusion of this book, which we hope will help bring you as much pleasure as we get from planting, owning, and sharing terrariums. Unlike our other project instructions, we don't think you have to stick to a set of rules for this final one, but perhaps you'll get some good ideas from our party. Just one word of caution — it may make you the most popular party-giver in town!

We chose a Sunday afternoon for our party because it allowed time for planting, with an informal light supper and conversation afterward. Of course, any time that suits you and your friends is fine. Don't get too involved with the food, though. No one expects you to prove that you are a terrarium expert and a gourmet chef on the same day. Something that can be cooked earlier and reheated or picnic-style food is best. We had beef stew, green salad, rolls, red wine, with strawberries in lemon yogurt for dessert.

195

Written invitations are a good idea, because there is specific information to be given.

You are invited to a terrarium planting party on Sunday, March 10, at 4:00 pm, 322 West 20th Street. Please bring a clear glass container with a capacity of 1½ to 2½ quarts, with an opening that allows you to reach inside. Be sure it has a lid or top. We will provide all other materials, including plants. Supper will follow the planting. Wear terrarium planting clothes.

As you can see from the invitation, this party was for friends who would be planting their first terrarium. We invited six guests, and even with two people giving instructions things sometimes got a little helter-skelter, but that was part of the fun. If you have plenty of work space more guests could be invited, maybe some who might just like to watch. If you have a group with a bit of terrarium experience you could have a bottle-garden or large-container planting party. For the bottle-garden party several sets of tools would be a good idea.

A shopping list for this party involves some rather large quantities, but as an advanced terrarium builder you may have many of the items around. This list is adequate for six beginner-sized terrariums.

Cleaning materials — glass cleaner and a roll of paper towels
Drainage — two quarts of gravel or pebbles
Charcoal — one-half cup
Soil separator — two square feet of fiber glass or other synthetic material
Sterilized potting soil — two quarts
Soil lightener — one and one half quarts of perlite or sand
Peat moss — one quart

Plants — all from the tropical category. For six terrariums we allowed eight medium (3- to 4-inch), twelve small (2- to 3-inch),
and eight ground-cover plants plus some moss. It's better to have
a few extra as you can't tell exactly what size containers people
will bring. This allows your guests to have a choice of plants; if
any are left over you have a start on a new terrarium for yourself.

Tools —

three large spoons

three tamping instruments

a pair of scissors, or two if possible

three mixing cups or other units that can be used for proportioning

three mixing bowls or inexpensive cardboard buckets from a paint
store

a watercolor brush for cleaning leaves

Natural decorative elements — provide a large selection so that your
friends can choose and design with them

Watering device — your bulb sprayer or plant mister

Be sure to assemble all elements on a work surface before your guests arrive

Planting may move slowly at first, but soon the enthusiasm will increase

You could offer your guests a light punch or coffee while you look over the containers that have been brought and generally get warmed up for planting. When everyone is ready, move to the assembly area. In our case this was a large table in a basement workshop. It's not very elegant but spills don't hurt. In warm weather this is a perfect outdoor party.

Before the guests arrive place all of the materials on the table. Try to set up three separate work areas, each for two people. Put the potting soil, perlite, and peat moss in big cardboard paint buckets and label the contents. Each pair of guests should have their own set of tools and equipment, except for scissors which can be shared.

We simply explained each of the ten basic terrarium planting steps as we went along, helping out with practical tips and showing ways to proceed. We checked to be sure enough drainage was used, demonstrated how to take plants out of pots, and gave similar assistance. It's important to explain the function of each element, such as the role of the soil separator in keeping the drainage level free of soil mix. As often happens, we learned a few things from our "students." One person who found it awkward to extract a plant from its pot by tapping the bottom with a spoon, easily removed it by giving it a thump with the palm of her hand.

Mostly, be prepared to give advice about plant placement, the use of natural elements, and soil-mix depth. We also measured out the correct amount of water to be used for moisture balance according to container size, but let the planters apply it. Be sure to have a correctly misting terrarium on hand, or show the three misting drawings on page 73. Advise your guests on light conditions and possible locations for their new terrariums. Don't forget to explain that the moisture balance must be adjusted after the terrarium is in its permanent location.

By this point everyone is totally absorbed in creating the best design possible

Completed terrariums and their proud owners

After the planting was completed and the watering done, we took all the terrariums to the dining area and used them as a centerpiece for the buffet table, which delighted everyone.

One final but important gesture — hand out small paper shopping bags so that everyone has a way of carrying his terrarium without tipping or spilling.

Best wishes for a great party and happy terrarium planting!

Ken Kayatta

Steven Schmidt

Sources
and Index

Sources

Containers

Ambassador All-Glass Aquariums Inc., Freeport, N.Y.
Manufacturers of aquariums in many shapes and sizes, available at most tropical fish stores.

Anchor Hocking Corporation, 199 N. Broad Street, Lancaster, Ohio, 43130
Manufacturers of a wide line of glass terrariums as well as storage jars, fish bowls, apothecary jars, etc.; widely distributed through discount stores and houseware sections of department stores.

Aquarium Stock Company Inc., 31 Warren Street, New York, N.Y., 10007
Retailers of fish tanks, and also some very unusual rocks, excellent for banking.

Christen, Inc., 59 Branch Street, St. Louis, Mo., 63147
Distributor of an excellently designed line of glass containers and some kits with soil and drainage materials. Especially outstanding are the mushroom, dome, and ball shapes. Widely distributed through garden centers and department stores.

Corning Glass Works, Corning, N.Y., 14830
Manufacturers of the "Creative Glassware" line. Distributed through kitchen specialty stores and houseware sections of department stores.

Cosas Designs, 44 Gough Street, San Francisco, Calif., 94103
Manufacturers of the plastic "Terrasphere" planter and some kits with soil and drainage materials. Available at most garden centers and plant stores.

Metaframe Corporation, 41 Slater Drive, East Paterson, N.J., 07407
Manufacturers of excellent all-glass aquariums plus sliding glass tops. Widely distributed through tropical fish stores and variety stores.

Midwestern Winemakers, 209 Roosevelt Road, Box 552, Cedar Falls, Iowa, 50613
Manufacturers of the Garden in a Bottle line, available in a kit form with soil mix, drainage materials, and terrarium tongs. Distributed through Montgomery Ward, J. C. Penney, Sears, Roebuck, and garden centers.

New Renaissance Glass Works, 5636 College Avenue, Oakland, Calif., 94618
Producers of a fine line of handcrafted, leaded glass terrariums, many resembling the old "Wardian Cases." Some also come in a do-it-yourself kit form. For catalog send 25¢ plus a self-addressed envelope.

O'Dell Manufacturing Inc., 1930 South 23rd Street, Saginaw, Mich., 48601
Manufacturers of aquarium tanks in many shapes and sizes. Widely distributed through most tropical fish stores.

Pilgrim Glass Corporation, Moonachie, New Jersey, 07074
Manufacturers of "Kitchen Chemistry" containers. Excellent designs in such shapes as milk bottles, apothecary jars, canisters, and flasks, available at most kitchen, specialty and gift stores, and houseware sections of department stores.

Riekes Crisa, Omaha, Nebraska, 68102
Manufacturers of hand-blown spheres, many sizes of bottles, domes, and many other containers. Widely distributed through most garden centers, plant stores, department stores, and variety stores.

Plants — All will ship mail order unless otherwise noted.

Allgrove (Arthur Eames), Box 459, North Wilmington, Mass., 01887
Grower and collector of woodland, tropical, and wildflower plants, and also some containers. Features an excellent partridgeberry bowl plant collection. Send 50¢ for an illustrated catalog.

Armstrong Associates Inc., Box 94, Kennebunk, Maine, 04043
The world's largest supplier of carnivorous plants. Many exotic varieties available, also some complete children's projects. Catalog on request.

Arndt's Floral Garden, 20453 N.E. Sandy Blvd., Troutdale, Oregon, 97060
Gesneriads and other small plants. List 10¢

Barrington Greenhouses, 860 Clemente Road, Barrington, N.J., 08016
A good selection of small terrarium plants. Catalog on request.

Beahm Gardens, 2686 Paloma Street, Pasadena, Calif., 91107
Cacti and succulents. List on request.

Buell's Greenhouses, Eastford, Conn., 06242
Gesneriads and other small plants. Catalog $1.00

Cactus by Mueller, 10411 Rosedale Highway, Bakersfield, Calif., 93307
  Cacti and succulents. List 10¢

Farm and Garden Nursery Inc., 116 Reade Street, New York, N.Y., 10013
  Wide selection of small plants, lights, and other accessories, including a miniature 3-piece terrarium tool set. No shipping or catalog.

Fischer Greenhouses, Linwood, N.J., 08221
  African violets and many other flowering plants. Catalog 25¢

Henrietta's Nursery, 1345 North Brawley Ave., Fresno, Calif., 93705
  Cacti and succulents. Catalog 50¢

Kartuz Greenhouses, 92 Chestnut Street, Wilmington, Mass., 01887
  A large selection of plants, especially flowering gesneriads. Catalog 50¢

Lager and Hurrel, 426 Morris Avenue, Summit, N.J., 07901
  A large growing operation specializing in orchids. Catalog $2.00

Lester, Robert, 280 West 4th Street, New York, N.Y., 10014
  Orchid specialist, with a fantastic collection of unusual and rare varieties. By appointment only. No shipping.

Merry Gardens, Camden, Maine, 04843
  Begonias and other plants, over 1500 different varieties, catalog $1.00

Wyrtzen Exotic Plants, 165 Bryant Avenue, Floral Park, N. Y., 11001
  Begonias, gesneriads and other plants. List on request.

Lights

Duro-Test Corp., 2321 Kennedy Blvd., North Bergen, N.J.
  Manufacturers of the "Vita-Lite" and "Naturescent," both widely distributed through garden centers, plant stores, electrical and hardware stores.

Floralite Co., 4124 E. Oakwood Rd., Oak Creek, Wis., 53154
  Fluorescent light units in many designs, catalog on request.

House Plant Corner, Box 165S, Oxford, Md., 21654
  Distributor of many kinds of indoor gardening equipment and supplies. Catalog 25¢

Jewel Electric Products Inc., 17–10 Willow Street, Fair Lawn, N.J., 07410
  Manufacturers of the "Super Lumen" mercury vapor bulbs, and the "Power Twist Vita Lite" fluorescent bulb. Available at most garden centers and plant stores.

Miscellaneous Suppliers

A&N Terrarium Tool Co., 5979 Hosta Lane, San Jose, Calif., 95124
  Producers of a 3 tool set, plus terrarium cutters especially designed for tall bottle gardens. Send for catalog.

Black Magic Inc., 530 Sixth Avenue, Hermosa Beach, Calif., 90254
  Distributors of a full range of soil and soil elements in many sizes, available at garden centers, plant stores, and some supermarkets.

Swiss Farms, Inc., Philmont, N.Y.
  Distributor of a full range of soil and soil elements, including a pre-packaged terrarium soil, available in many sizes. Distributed through major variety stores, garden centers, plant stores, hardware stores, and supermarkets.

Index

Numbers in italics refer to photographs.

I

Infusoria, 150
Insect-eating (carnivorous) plants,
    177–81
      for children, 192
      feeding, 182–83
Insects, 138–40
Insect spray, 139
Iresine (Bloodleaf), 49

J

Jade Plant (Crassula), 61

K

Kalanchoe, 62

L

Lamps
    fluorescent, 163–64
    incandescent, 164–67
Leaf mold, 41
    in mixes, 44
Lichen, 57
Light, artificial. *See* Artificial Light
Light conditions, 17, *18*
Limestone, 42
    in mixes, 43–44
Live-for-ever (Sempervivum), 63
Lizards, 147, 149, *142*, *145*. *See also*
  individual animal names
Lobivia (Cob Cactus), 58
Lycopodium (Club Moss), 57

M

Maidenhair Fern (*Adiantum*), 56
Maintenance, routine, 133–38
Mammillaria (Pincushion or Powder-
    puff Cactus), 60
Maranta (Prayer Plant), 50
Mealworms, 147
Mealybugs, 139
Mechanical grabber, 103, 104, 108
Mercury vapor bulb, 166–67, *167*
Mildew, 140
Mimosa (*Mimosa pudica*), 52

Miniature terrarium, 82–83, *82*, *83*
Misting guide, 73
Mitchella repens (Partridgeberry), 53
Mites, 139–40
Moisture balance, 72, 73, 131, 133–34
    in bottle garden, 111
Mold, 140, *140*
Moss, 57, 122
Mother-of-thousands (*Saxifraga sar-
    mentosa*), 51
Mover (tool), 104

N

Narrow-neck Terrariums. *See* Bottle
  gardens
Natural decorative elements, 76, 121,
    122, *123*
      Sterilizing, 69, 121–22
Neanthe bella (Parlor Palm), 50
Nephrolepis exaltata (Fluffy Ruffles
    Fern), 55
New England Partridgeberry Bowls,
    78, *79*
Newts, 145, 151–52
Night Lizards, 149
Norfolk Island Pine (*Araucaria*), 53
Notocactus (Ball Cactus), 58

O

Old Man Cactus (*Cephalocereus se-
    nilis*), 60
Opuntia (Prickly Pear), 60
Orchids, 172

P

Pachyphytum, 62
Panda Plant (*Kalanchoe tomentosa*),
    62
Parlor Palm (*Chamaedorea*), 50
Partridgeberry (*Mitchella repens*), 53
Partridgeberry bowls, 78, *79*
Peanut Cactus (*Chamaecereus silves-
    tri*), 59
Peat Moss, 40
    in soil mixes, 43–44
Pellaea rotundifolia (Cliffbrake Fern),
    55